Presented To:

_____

From:

_____

Simply Pray

A Prayer Resource for Couples and Singles including 3 Secret Weapons for a Strong Marriage and Family

**Minister Brian
& Michelle Gines**

Purpose Publishing
13194 US Highway 301 S
Riverview, FL 33578
www.PurposePublishing.com

Simply Pray
Copyright © 2021 by Brian & Michelle Gines
ISBN: 9781087959351

Bulk Ordering Information: Quantity sales. Special discounts are available on quantity purchases by churches, ministry associations, and others. For details, contact the author at marraige@ newlifeinchrist.net.

For details and to join our Marriage & Family community, reach out by email to michellegines60@gmail.com. We work with couples and groups, online and in-person, with our proprietary program Marriage CEO. However, due to the divine nature and success of the program we now work with only with selected entities. You can reach out expressing interest in the application process and details. We look forward to serving your ministry and marriage.

Dedication

The Heart 2 Heart Marriage Ministry of New Life in Christ International Ministries It has been our work in this ministry that has encouraged us to look at, increase, and prioritize our prayer life as individuals and together. Thank you to the H2H team. We have had the pleasure of working alongside these married couples. It has been a pleasure to serve with you all. With sincere hearts, we thank you all for encouraging us to share our imperfect lives in transparent ways and receiving us.

Apostle Keith and Pastor Lisa Wesley You have been an inspiration to us in marriage. Because you saw something in us, you gave us the opportunity to find a place of grace in ministry together. Thank you for entrusting us to such a work of God.

Sis Bobbie Saulsberry and the New Life in Christ S.W.A.T. Prayer Ministry Your diligence, passion, and earnest pursuit of God in prayer has not only taught us, but pushed and challenged us to go deeper, stay on the wall, and fight the good fight in prayer.

Our Parents The seeds you all planted in us have made our love for God and His people a priority. We thank you for your love, your support, your prayers, your encouragement, and your marriages. Through it all, ups and downs, the good and the bad, staying together or living through divorce- we have been able to learn from you. The two of us are better because of who we had as examples in our lives.

Our Children Zerryn, Brielle, and Charis, you all are our greatest inspiration for loving God and each other more fully. It's encouraging for us to see the young adults you've become and are still becoming. Our marriage is enriched by seeing the beautiful fruit we are honored to call, our children.

Married Couples You are the biggest part of *Simply Pray*. It is because of the countless husbands and wives that we know and don't know that need support. It is our heartfelt prayer that within these pages you find strength, words, and rest in the arms of God. It is through prayer that we found the fuel we needed to battle the enemy God's way and without doubting. We want you to find that too.

Foreword
by Elder Bobbie Saulsberry

It has been a great joy to read this book, and even greater honor to write the foreword. Let me share a little on the Gines, Brian and Michelle, they are hidden gems, treasures not revealed. They are a precious find, treasure in an earthen vessel. I believe that they are a couple given to the fullness of the Word of God, in their home with their family, their in laws, their personal relationship with each other and to their Church. They are an example of Christ and the Church.

I have read several books on prayer, this book "Simply Pray" a prayer resource created for couples is excellent. It has structure built into it, if you were to put this book to test, you would become richer in your prayer life with God and in your relationship with your spouse, your children, and people in general.

Although it is written to couples, it so well written, with applicable scriptures, structures, and suggestions to pray that singles would benefit in preparing for their future spouses.

It gives you 31 days of prayer devotions, a section on affirming each other and your children. The third section is targeted prayers to help you reach out pass your comfort zone and bring others before the Father.

The section on Affirmation is powerful, because we are speaking spirits, our words have power, we can shape a person to believe what he may not be at that moment, and our words affect them. *A word fitly spoken is like apples of gold in pictures of silver. (Proverbs 25:11KJV)*

Targeting prayers for everything, will increase the wealth of God in you, praying for others empowers you, and strengthens you. This book is worth your investing in it to read it, study it and do it. I encourage you to invest in this book in the soul of your marriage, your relationships and you will come out stronger, fortified and strengthened in your prayer life and everything that is connected to you.

Treat its content as treasure that you have found, because it is treasure that has been hidden but now revealed.

Thank you, Brian & Michelle for this honor!

Bobbie Saulsberry,
S.W.A.T. Prayer Ministry Leader
New Life in Christ International Ministries

Table of Contents

A Note from the Authors
The Minister and the Mrs.

All marriages have an enemy. The enemy who wants to steal, kill, destroy, and devour your marriage. One of the most powerful weapons you have is prayer. We say that prayer is our Dragon Slayer. We use prayer as a weapon against the enemy on behalf of each other, our children, our families, our church, our communities, and our nation.

You cannot fight a spiritual battle using physical weapons. It is funny how easy it is to quarrel with your spouse, rather than ending the quarrel by embracing God as your helper against the enemy. Or how easy it is to complain to a friend or family member rather than to bring your complaint to God instead? How easy it is to worry about issues rather than pray about them. What if we turned all the quarrels, complaints, and worries into prayers? Can I tell you that the victory, the peace, and the blessing it is for all of us is immeasurable when we take this approach.

We encourage all of you along with us to pray because prayers are a powerful weapon. Prayers make a difference. Pray from a place of faith, not fear. Even if you are single person, pray for your *will-be* spouse and marriage.

Continue earnestly in prayer, being vigilant in it with thanksgiving. (Colossians 4:2 NKJV). We cannot afford not to pray. We cannot survive without praying. Prayer is our lifeline. Remember, let prayer be *your* Dragon Slayer. It eases the tension and the fear when you commit first to prayer as the **first** option, not your last resort.

Be anxious for nothing, but in everything by prayer and supplication, with thanksgiving, let your requests be made known to God. (Philippians 4:6 NKJV)

The ultimate key to spiritual growth for adults and in marriage is spending time **alone** with God. This means taking the time to speak with God about whatever is on your heart and, even more importantly, allowing Him to speak to you concerning your spouse, your finances, your children, your fears, your dreams, and everything that concerns you.

Let us bring up another point you might not have considered. What about just talking to God and telling him about all the *great* things happening in your life? Do you know how excited He would be for your grateful heart? Along with that, it'll be easier for you to maintain the relationship of communication with him when you share all of it with Him, good and bad.

One of the most deceiving lies of the enemy is that we don't have to pray. And the truth is no one ever says out loud, "I don't need to pray," we just don't do it. However, all of us have enough time to talk on our cell phones, search the internet, and tweet. We would be amazed at how much more time is available to us for prayer if we spent less time on doing other things. We don't want to get into any debates about how anyone spends their time, but we encourage you to take some **intentional time** away from your device to devote a little more time to prayer. I believe that things will be better when we can focus on the love, we have for each other rather than spending too much time in the habit of things other than prayer. There's no set formula on how often, how long, or how much we share in prayer. The time you devote in prayer will yield fruit in many ways.

We must be willing to wait in the Lord's presence until we receive God's directives or His words of consolation, especially for our spouse. *Our spouse is worth it. Our relationship is worth it. Our marriage is worth it.*

The power of prayer is not the result of the person praying. Rather, the power resides in the God who is being prayed to—Our Heavenly Father. In the scripture, 1 John 5:14-15 he declares, *this is the confidence we have in approaching God: that if we ask anything according to His will, he hears us. If we know that He hears us—whatever we ask—we know that we have what we asked of Him (NIV).* No matter the person praying, the passion behind the prayers, or the purpose of the prayer—God answers prayers that agree with His will. God's answers are not always yes, nor based on our timetable. But He always answers in our best interest and the best interest of your husband or wife. You must be open and listen for His voice. Sometimes His voice will conflict with yours and that's when you must really be open to doing His will and not your own. After all, you can trust your relationship will be the better for it.

After many years of serving God together, we present to you *Simply Pray* as a resource, tool, and strategy to win the war over the enemy through prayer. Be mindful that we are being transparent and sharing with you the secrets of our warfare. No war is ever won without battle being won first in the *spirit*. In addition, no war is won without having to fight. It's sometimes a hard fight, a long fight, a knock down or drag out fight, but a fight, nonetheless. The beautiful thing is that what you fight in prayer, you win in your walk and witness before others.

But through it all, there is a God who we serve who has our backs and gives us the victory. Jesus intercedes for us and the Holy Spirit is our advocate and guide inside of us. Together, you and your spouse will be empowered to go to God, in His language (the Word), and win every battle over all the enemies of this world.

There are many tools' Gods equips us with to battle the enemy. We've chosen prayer as a weapon to expand on at this time. *Prayer is our Dragon Slayer!* There is so much for us to pray about and beseech the Lord on behalf of our families, our friends, ourselves, but more importantly our spouses. We pray that you find this book a blessing and some help.

God Bless you and your spouse!

Introduction

The concept of communicating with God—talking directly and openly with Him is just as we would talk with an intimate friend. Once started, it is one of the greatest experiences of the Christian life. Just as one key to quality relationships is time spent effectively communicating with each other, so is growing a personal relationship with Him in prayer and hearing His voice in Scripture. Romans 10:17 says, *Faith comes by hearing, and hearing by the word of God (NKJV).*

Most of us want to pray more than we do, but we often find our prayers are sporadic and unanswered. *Simply Pray* was designed to make prayer a more enriching and satisfying experience by providing both form and freedom. The form is the scripture itself, and the freedom is your own thoughts and prayers in response to the truth in scripture. Additionally, we've placed a section of delicately prepared prayers on specific topics and specific people in your life that allow you to make the prayers your own in response to a need. Since there are many, many, many things we need and ought to pray for; this is not an exhaustive list. But we did include ones we've found to be impactful on our marriage.

A problem some find with prayer is that it is easy to slip into extreme form and no freedom. Or the opposite extreme of all freedom and no form. Mere form leads to a rote or impersonal approach to prayer, while mere freedom produces unbalanced and undisciplined prayer life that can degenerate into a series of one 'gimme' after another.

Simply Pray is a tool that guides you through the process of praying His Word back to God. This enables you to think God's thoughts and personalize them in your own words. It also provides a balanced diet of prayer by leading you through different kinds of prayer. Because it based on scripture, your prayers will be pleasing to God. The knowledge, but more importantly the experience, will encourage you even more in your daily time alone with God.

Structure of Simply Pray

Simply Pray includes 3 sections that make up the entire book. We believe that it is important to consider what helps us make our prayers most effective and will help you even when you don't have words of your own. We've provided a little help and inspiration.

The three sections are:

- 31 Days of Prayer
- Affirmations
- Targeted Prayers

Jesus' great commandment for all of us as believers is *You shall love the LORD your God with all your heart, with all your soul, and with all your mind. This is the first and great commandment. And the second is like it: You shall love your neighbor as yourself* (Matthew 22:37-39 NKJV). Our prayers extend our love back to God and enables us to love others.

Prepare 'Me & My Heart' for Prayer
An Activity

Now, as a prerequisite exercise we are going to take time in this section to discuss the importance and significance of confessing our sins to God. We do not want anything to hinder our prayers, so we must begin with what the Bible tells us as husbands and wives regarding prayer. In Peter's first letter he mentions prayer three times. What is remarkable about these three instances is that there is a familiar tone in each of them. Let's read them here below and see if you can detect the common thread running through each.

First, Peter has a word for husbands about prayer and their relationship with their wives: *"You husbands likewise, live with your wives in an understanding way, as with a weaker vessel, since she is a woman; and grant her honor as a fellow heir of the grace of life, so that your prayers may not be hindered."* (1 Peter 3:7 **KJV**).

Second, in the very next paragraph he speaks to all believers (verse 8) about being brotherly and kindhearted and humble and (verse 9) not returning evil for evil but instead giving a blessing. Then, to support these admonitions he quotes *"Let him who means to love life and see good days refrain his tongue from evil and his lips from speaking guile. And let him turn away from evil and do good; let him seek peace and pursue it. For the eyes of the Lord are upon the righteous, and his ears attend to their prayer, but the face of the Lord is against those who do evil."* (1 Pet 3:10–12 **KJV**).

Third, in (1 Peter 4:7 **KJV**), he says, *"The end of all things is at hand; therefore, be of sound judgment and sober spirit for the purpose of prayer {literally: for the sake of prayers}."*

Now, did you see the common thread running through those three references to prayer? What struck me is that all three teach us not only that praying helps us live right, but that living right also helps us pray. Our goal here is to ensure that as a married couple to keep your hearts clean and remove any hindrances to our prayers. This is our why we seek to have a clean heart when we pray.

Now, here are a few specific scriptures that speak to *keeping* our hearts clean before God and keeping our prayers from being hindered. This is *how* we do it. Before you begin praying if you have things in your heart, release them. Recite each of these scriptures to allow the flow of communication from you unto the Lord to remain open, flowing, and unobstructed. You can make them personal by inserting your name or the correct pronoun to give you ownership in this confession of heart.

As well, these are some specific scriptures to recite aloud before you begin to pray when *you know* that your heart needs cleansing. As you will see, without taking this critical step it's easy to forfeit the best that God has for you and your spouse. Remember the goal with this exercise is to ensure that there is nothing separating you from God that would hinder your prayers from getting through. Recite these prayers aloud now to bring them into your conscious focus and memory.

Psalm 51:10 (NIV)

Create in me a pure heart, O God, and renew a steadfast spirit within me.

1 John 1:9 (NIV)

"If we confess our sins, he is faithful and just and will forgive us our sins and purify us from all unrighteousness."

Jesus clarifies that sin begins in our hearts and includes our thoughts, not *only* our words and actions.

We've talked about prayer being a weapon against the enemy, but it's also one of the ways God has appointed to help us live the way we should. And to Peter's point in every one of the verses is that it's true the other way around: God has appointed a way for us to live which will help us pray. There are ways to live that hinder prayer and there is a way to live that helps prayer. We want to focus this exercise on helping our prayers through confessing our sins and preparing our hearts first. This is sometimes referred to as posturing ourselves for prayer. Let's begin another exercise by praying these prayers below. We are taking God's Word and making it your own to the glory of God.

1. **Lord, I thank you for my spouse that you blessed me with. I know that** *Whatever is good and perfect comes down to us from God our Father, who created all the lights in the heavens.* (James 1: 17 NLT) and I am grateful to you for my blessing. And I will *Be thankful in all circumstances, for this is God's will for (me) who belongs to Christ Jesus.* (1 Thessalonians 5:18 NLT)

2. **Lord, I ask for your help to be forgiving and lovingly tolerant towards my husband/ wife. Your word says** *Make allowance for each other's faults and forgive anyone who offends you. Remember, the Lord forgave you, so you must forgive others.* (Colossians 3:13 NLT) and I will do as your Word commands.

3. Lord, help me to love my spouse uncondi-
tionally just as you love me. I believe your
Word that says, "*Love is patient and kind. Love
is not jealous or boastful or proud or rude. It does
not demand its own way. It is not irritable, and it
keeps no record of being wronged. It does not rejoice
about injustice but rejoices whenever the truth wins
out. Love never gives up, never loses faith, is always
hopeful, and endures through every circumstance.*" (1
Corinthians 13:4-7 NLT). I receive and trust
this as my personal view of loving my spouse.

4. Father, help me to encourage my spouse
fulfill your plan for his/her life. Your Word
says, "*I knew you before I formed you in your mother's womb. Before you were born, I set you apart and
appointed you as my prophet to the nations.*" (Jeremiah 1:5 NLT). This is our personal prayer for
my spouse to be all you have called him/her to
be. I will support and provoke him/her to love
and good works for you.

5. Lord, let my spouse and I seek you first
before anyone or other thing else. We will
"*seek the Kingdom of God above all else, and live
righteously, and you will give us everything we
need.*" (Matthew 6:33 NLT). As a family unit,
we will be as Joshua and say, "*But as for me
and my family, we will serve the LORD.*" (Joshua
24:15 NLT).

6. Lord, teach us to depend on your power through every difficult moment we face together. We "*... understand the incredible greatness of God's power for us who believe him.*" (Ephesians 1:19 NLT) and confess God's Word.

7. Lord help me bridle my tongue and not say hurtful things to my spouse. *"Let your speech always be gracious, seasoned with salt, so that you may know how you ought to answer each person."* (Colossians 4:6 ESV)

8. Lord help my spouse and I to not yield to any temptation that may come our way. *"The temptations in your life are no different from what others experience. And God is faithful. He will not allow the temptation to be more than you can stand. When you are tempted, he will show you a way out so that you can endure."* (1 Corinthians 10:13 NLT)

9. Lord, separate my spouse and me from every evil company. *"Do not be deceived: 'Bad company ruins good morals.'"* (1 Corinthians 15:33 ESV)

10. Lord, let your peace reign in our home. *"Then you will experience God's peace, which exceeds anything we can understand. His peace will guard your hearts and minds as you live in Christ Jesus."* (Philippians 4:7 NLT)

SECTION 1

31 Days of Simply Pray Devotionals

imply Pray begins with a devotional section to bring you and your spouse together around the Word of God and towards each other. This section is especially called out to engage in the exercise of communing with God as a couple around topics and thoughts that matter to you both. Devotion to God implies ardent affection for him -- a yielding of the heart to him with reverence, faith, and piety in every act, particularly in prayer and meditation in His Word. As you grow in your understanding of who God is, who you both are as His children and how together you can slay your dragons through dedicated and regular times of devotion. You will be able to love and serve God and others as He has called us all to do.

There are *31 Days of Simply Pray Devotional Topics* that you can adapt to your schedule that best fit your life.

We understand that couples have a lot on their plates and time together must be carved out, regularly. This is part of the required action you'll need to take as a couple to see your marriage come into or stay in agreement over time. They can be used profitably in a short period of time (15-30 minutes), or you can move through them more slowly (1 hour), as you see fit. Although you can tie these daily prayers to the day of the month, there is no need to do so, particularly if you find yourself needing a moment with God at any time. But you may decide to mark your place and pick up where you left off. As well, you may find that moving from topic to topic can be strengthening as you find specific areas of need. Either way, we know and believe that once you commit to doing this together-you won't stop. It'll become a habit that's sure to bring honor to God and blessings to your marriage and family.

Our System for Success

We begin with a topic, followed by an applicable scripture. We then illustrate the point of the message and context through a story, example or experience that further brings insight for you and your spouse. We end with a His & Her question and answer section. This allows you and your spouse to discuss and share. We conclude each devotion with a simple prayer. If you're unfamiliar with the scripture, take the time to pull out your Bible to look up the reference or even a different translation. This will enable you to get a better grasp on the concept being presented. We want to encourage you to use the Word as a place of reference for all that this book uses to equip you on your journey.

Consider using the space in the margin and spaces of this book to add your own thoughts and prayers as they come. There is also a His & Hers section on the sides each page especially designed for prayer concerns and documenting answered prayer. This may not be the first time you've seen this style of notation in a book, but we created this for you and your spouse to hear the silent cries of each other's heart that may not be easily spoken. But you can join one another in agreement, prayer, and intercession in a way to honor one another and each other's personal prayer requests. It's not set up to be a place of division, but rather to be unified in slaying the dragon together even when it may appear that your thoughts are very different. It's good to see and hear where each of you are and join one another in seeking God for the answer in strength rather than alone in weakness. Many times, over the years my spouse and I may have felt at odds with one another about one thing or another. But we found that our hearts were always for God and His plan for our lives even when we couldn't really communicate that to each other. In this place, you can record a list of prayers for yourself and for your marriage.

Scripture Versions Disclaimer

We created this collection of biblical devotions, affirmations and prayers using multiple translations. Our intention in doing this was to remain as close to the biblical text as possible, while retaining clarity and readability around a subject. You'll see in the affirmation area that when teaching children to affirm themselves, we use scriptures from the New International Version which makes understanding a little simpler for children to understand. Of course, you're always free and able to look up any referenced scripture in the version you find most preferred.

1

Our Holy Third Party

*For other foundation can no man lay
than that is laid, which is Jesus Christ.*
(1 Corinthians 3:11KJV)

To experience genuine love with our mate, we must bring a third party into the equation—Jesus Christ. Only through this spiritual connection with Him can we begin to fulfill all the potential of the relationship we call marriage.

Anyone who studies the Bible will recognize numerous principles woven throughout that apply to married life. Judeo Christian values have effectively guided men and women from the beginning. These values were inspired by the Creator Himself, the originator of the institution of marriage. No matter what society says, or how laws may change, the precepts that make up this scriptural system remain the way to find love and happiness in life.

Establishing a personal relationship with Jesus Christ is the critical first step toward attaining every meaningful goal, including the intimacy we all seek. If you haven't already given your heart to Him, we urge you to do so. It will bring meaning and purpose to every dimension of your life—including your marriage. Tomorrow we'll explain how.

His & Her Discussion Questions

- How have we been putting biblical principles to work in our marriage?
- How can I encourage you to spend more time in God's Word?
- Have we both personally invited Jesus Christ to be Lord of our lives and of our marriage? If not, can we take that life changing step right now?

Our Prayer

Lord Jesus, You are the foundation of our marriage. Help us look to You and Your strength in every way as we build a life together. Amen.

2

Every Day & Little Things

"I was filled with delight day after day."
(Proverbs 8:30 NIV)

We all cherish the events during our married lives: the wedding and honeymoon, childbirth, the 1st and 20th wedding anniversaries, Kindergarten, high school, and the college graduations.

It is needful for us to celebrate these momentous occasions and hug, kiss, take pictures and send congratulations to all. But we must not forget to savor the everyday and little things that account for the rest of the days of our lives. Consider the meaning of waking up each morning next to the boy you sat next to in fourth grade. Can you believe that this someone you love and to begin each day with. . .? you exchange quick glances with your partner as you teach together or share a cup of coffee . . . to hold hands with your mate in church as you sing praises to our glorious God? When you review the mental scrapbook of images from your marriage, we hope it is filled with happy memories of the "big moments" you've shared together. But also, be sure to include snapshots of those joyful, everyday events that make each day of marriage something special.

His & Her Discussion Questions

- What everyday activities bring you joy?
- Do you think we have lived from one big event to the next—or have we tried to make ordinary days special, too?
- How can we help each other savor everyday moments?
- Do our lives demonstrate to others that each moment is a gift from God?

Our Prayer

Father, we find Your love in the simple joys around us—a bird's song or a smile from our mate, blue skies, or the laughter of children. Thank You for health and for Your unfailing abundance. Open our eyes to the wealth of each day, o Lord. May we never live like paupers when You have made us so rich. Amen.

3

SOMEONE IS LISTENING

{The righteous} are always generous and
lend freely; their children will be blessed.
(Psalm 37:26 NIV)

B e careful what you say in the presence of your
babies. That's the advice of a researcher at
Johns Hopkins University, who tells us that children only eight months of age are capable of hearing
and remembering words, good and bad. In a study
by Dr. Peter Juscyzk, babies were exposed to three
recorded stories for a period of about ten days. When
they were tested in the lab two weeks later, they
clearly recognized the words in the stories but failed
to respond to those they hadn't heard. According
to Robin Chapman, a University of Wisconsin language specialist, the study demonstrates that very
young children attend to the sounds of language
and can pick out those that are familiar. Chapman

concludes that "a lot of language learning is happening in the first year of life."[1]

Whether we like it or not, almost everything we say and do is observed and recorded—by the patrolman with a radar gun, by the convenience store video camera, and even by our young children. If our marriage models a spirit of generosity worth imitating, it will lead to blessings for everyone.

His & Her Discussion Questions

- What are some of your earliest memories of your parents' words and actions?
- If we videotaped ourselves, would we be pleased by what we saw?
- Besides each other, whom do we influence with our everyday words and deeds? Are we modeling a spirit of generosity for them?

Our Prayer

Lord, we know that our every action has a tremendous impact on those around us, and we want to be mature, responsible, and positive ambassadors for You. Help us glorify You in how we think, act, and speak. Amen.

---

[1] Language research and comments from "Infants' Memory for Spoken Words" by P. W. Juscyzk and E. A. Hohne (Science, 26 September 1997) and "Parents Beware: Little Ears Are Listening" by Rachel Ellis (Associated Press, http://www.ap.org/, 26 September 1997).

4

TAKING CHANCES

The righteous are as bold as a lion.
(Proverbs 28:1 KJV)

Remember Evel Knievel, the death defying dare-devil who jumped over cars, trucks, and all manner of objects on his motorcycle? Evel may have been a little too ambitious for his own good—he broke several bones in the process—but he can teach us something about risk.

When we stretch ourselves beyond our comfort zone, we experience the thrill and confidence that comes from facing a new challenge. In the case of a bored husband or wife, this may mean joining a speaker's group, volunteering to lead a Bible study, going on a backpacking trip, or taking a class. It might also include opening to your spouse or relating the message of Jesus to a group of nonbelievers. For me (JCD), it was leaving a comfortable position as a professor of pediatrics, where I had a predictable income and the support of a large university. I traded that for a little two room office and called it "Focus on the Family." Only God knew where that radical decision would lead, but it was the beginning of a ride that has resulted in my words being heard worldwide by two hundred million people every day. It was worth the risk, I would say.

Even if you don't do as well as you'd hoped, you'll still feel a sense of fulfillment from reaching for a dream. Just try not to break any bones.

His & Her Discussion Questions

- What kind of positive risks have we taken in our marriage?
- What risks does the Lord want us to avoid?
- What have you always wanted to do, but haven't yet dared to try?
- In what ways can we take a risk for Jesus Christ?

Our Prayer

Heavenly Father, we never want fear or complacency in our marriage. By the strength of Your Spirit, may we reach together for new challenges in faith as long as we live. Amen.

5

NEWLYWED NONSENSE

"Where is the respect due me?"
(Malachi 1:6 NIV)

Years ago, there was a TV game show called "The Newlywed Game". I caught an old episode flipping through the TV channels recently and I paused momentarily to watch it. It was a bad decision. The host posed a series of silly questions to a lineup of brides whose husbands were "sequestered backstage in a soundproof room."

The host challenged the women to predict their husband's responses to inquiries that went something like this: "Using the TV terms 'first run,' 'rerun,' or 'cancelled,' how would you describe the first time you and your husband made 'whoopee'?" Without the least hesitation, the women blurted out frank answers to this and other intimate questions. A few minutes later the men were given the same opportunity to humiliate their wives. Of course, they grabbed it.

It has been said that TV programming reflects the values of the society it serves. Heaven help us if that is true. In this instance, the newlyweds revealed their immaturity, selfishness, hostility, vulnerability, and sense of inadequacy. Rather than treat their sexual relationships— and each other—with the privacy and respect they deserved, these young marrieds aired every intimate detail to a national television audience without a second thought.

Intimacy will never be achieved in the bedroom, or in any part of the marriage, when the relationship is handled in so cavalier a manner. Some facts about your life together are best kept between you and your mate.

His & Her Discussion Questions

- Do you feel I respect our sexual relationship?
- Do I ever reveal details about our sex life you wish I didn't?
- How can the behavior described above damage a relationship?

Our Prayer

Lord, thank You for the intimacy that we share. May we be quick to recognize and reject popular values that offend You and our marriage commitment. Amen.

6

A LIGHTHEARTED SPIRIT

May the God of hope fill you with joy and peace as you trust in him, so that you may overflow with hope by the power of the Holy Spirit. (Romans 15:13 NIV)

As Christians who want to bring joy to our marriages, we might do well to remember that the Bible says, *"A cheerful heart is good medicine, but a crushed spirit dries up the bones."* (Proverbs 17:22 NIV) It's how we look at circumstances that makes all the difference. I like to say change the way you look at things and things will change the way they look.

For Christians, it's not just how we look at things; it's at Whom we're looking. *Rejoice in the Lord and be glad,* wrote David (Psalm 32:11). Paul gave the same advice to the Philippians. And the author of Hebrews wrote: *Let us fix our eyes on Jesus, the author and perfecter of our faith, who for the joy set before him endured the cross.* . . (Hebrews 12:2). Couples who keep Jesus Christ as Lord of their home seem to laugh more often and cultivate hope in their marriages more easily. Why? Because when Jesus carries the weight of your worries, your needs, and your future, lighthearted living is the natural result.

God gave us a sense of humor to help us stay pleasant in our marriage, and surely, He wants us to use and enjoy it!

His & Her Discussion Questions

- Do you think Jesus often laughed?
- Do you think we would laugh more if we trusted God more?
- What steps can we take to bring a lighthearted spirit into our home?
- How can we worship God by our attitudes about life's little hassles?

Our Prayer

Most amazing God, thank You for making humor possible in our world. Forgive us when selfishness, fear, or faithlessness rob us of laughter. Amen.

7

WHAT'D YOU SAY?

Let the wise listen and add to their learning.
(Proverbs 1:5 NIV)

Men may use less speech than women, but both sexes have been accused of not using their sense of hearing. "You never told me that" is a common household refrain. I heard a funny story about a preacher preaching at a revival tent meeting. During his sermon, an alley cat somehow decided to take a nap right on the platform. This preacher, who was 6'4", took a step backward and planted his heel squarely on the poor cat's tail. The cat went crazy, scratching and clawing to free himself. But the preacher not deterred by any devil or cat, stayed intent on his message, and didn't even notice. He later said he thought the screech came from the brakes of automobiles at a nearby stop sign. When my father finally moved his foot, the cat took off like a Saturn rocket.

This story illustrates the communication problem many couples face.

For example, a wife "screams" for attention and intimacy but feels that he doesn't even notice. It's not that he can't hear her; it's that he's thinking about something else or is completely misinterpreting her signals. This situation can easily be improved by simply "tuning in" to the station on which your mate is broadcasting. The truth is that careful listening feels so much like love that most of us can hardly tell the difference.

His & Her Discussion Questions

- When we tell each other something that doesn't get through, who is to blame—the "sender," the "receiver," or both?
- What have you wanted to say, but didn't because you couldn't get my attention?
- How could learning to listen better to each other help us listen better to God?

Our Prayer

Dear God, teach us the wisdom and grace of listening. Help us to pay attention to each word as though we were listening to You. Amen.

8

I PROMISE

"Simply let your 'Yes' be 'Yes,' and your 'No,' 'No.'" (Matthew 5:37 NKJV)

Love can be defined in myriad ways, but in marriage "I love you" really means "I promise to be there for you all of my days." It is a promise that says, "I'll be there when you lose your job, your health, your parents, your looks, your confidence, your friends." It's a promise that tells your partner, "I'll build you up; I'll overlook your weaknesses; I'll forgive your mistakes; I'll put your needs above my own; I'll stick by you even when the going gets tough."

This kind of assurance will hold you steady through all of life's ups and downs, through all the "better or worse" conditions.

The Lord has demonstrated throughout the ages that He keeps His promises—including the most important one of all, reserving a spot in heaven for each of His followers, for all eternity. Since God keeps

His promises, we must keep ours too—especially the one we made before God, our family, our friends, and our church on our wedding day.

His & Her Discussion Questions

- What part of my wedding vow means the most to you now?
- In what ways has our pledge to "stick together no matter what" seen us through hard times?
- How do we benefit spiritually from keeping our commitments?

Our Prayer

Dear Lord, give us Your strength today to honor our promises. May our word be our bond—to each other, to our friends, and to family and associates. Thank You that You never waiver on Your promises to us! Amen.

9

BIG BRIDGES

> *The winds blew and beat against that*
> *house; yet it did not fall, because it had*
> *its foundation on the rock.*
> (Matthew 7:25 NIV)

Yesterday we talked about being committed to your partner for better and for worse. Another way to look at this issue was once related by the late Dr. Francis Schaeffer. He described the bridges that were built in Europe by the Romans in the first and second centuries A.D. The bridges still stand today, despite the unreinforced brick and mortar with which they were made, because they are used for nothing but foot traffic. If an eighteen wheel semi were driven across those historic structures, they would crumble in a cloud of dust and debris.

Marriages that lack an iron willed determination to hang together are like those Roman bridges. They appear to be secure and may indeed remain upright for many years—until they are put under heavy pressure. Then the supports split and the structure crumbles.

Is your marriage constructed to withstand unusual stress as well as normal wear? Take the time to install a proper foundation—the Lord Jesus Christ. Then build your relationship on habits and attitudes that will sustain it under heavy pressure.

His & Her Discussion Questions

- Has there ever been a time when our marriage seemed less than solid?
- Do we know a couple whose marriage has stayed secure under stress?
- What's their secret?
- Do we see any cracks—even tiny ones—beginning to appear in our marriage?
- What can we do to repair them?

Our Prayer

Father, we turn to the unshakable truths of Your Word and the unfailing promise of Your presence to hold our marriage together. Thank You that we can live and love securely— even under stress—because You are in this marriage with us. Amen.

10

CONTROL YOUR ATTITUDE

Your attitude should be the same as that
of Jesus Christ.
(Philippians 2:5 NIV)

One morning, the late Bishop Fulton Sheen entered a greasy spoon for breakfast. "Bring me some ham and eggs and a few kind words for the day," he said.

The waitress returned fifteen minutes later and set the food before him. "There," she said. "What about the kind words?" he asked. She looked him over and replied, "I'd advise you not to eat those eggs!" Sometimes the first few events of the day make it clear it's going to be a "downer." No matter what you do, you can't stop life's bad turns: the car that rear ends yours on the way to work; the traffic jam that causes you to miss an important appointment. Yet you can choose your reaction to such irritating events.

We can live happily despite the ups and downs of everyday living, but to do so takes a great measure of dependence on Jesus Christ. The apostle Paul said it best: "I know what it is to be in need, and I know what it is to have plenty. I have learned the secret of being content in any and every situation, whether well fed or hungry, whether living in plenty or in want. I can do everything through Him who gives me strength." (Philippians 4:12–13).

His & Her Discussion Questions

- Am I generally cheerful and optimistic—or gloomy and pessimistic?
- How do I usually react when I'm disappointed or discouraged?
- How do my mood swings affect you and our marriage? How can we respond more positively to difficult events?

Our Prayer

Dear Father, we invite You to be at work in us—individually and in our relationship—to grow in us the same attitude as Jesus Christ. We don't want to be ruled by circumstances or moods but by Your Spirit. Amen.

11

DUE HONOR

Humility comes before honor.
(Proverbs 18:12 NIV)

Funny story, Old Mr. Smith learned that his neighbor, Mr. Jones, had presented flowers and a gift to Mrs. Jones five nights in a row. He thought, that must be what wins a woman's heart. So, Smith went out and bought a big box of candy and a bouquet of his wife's favorite flowers. Arriving home, a little early that after noon, he rang the doorbell. When Mrs. Smith appeared, he passionately embraced her. Suddenly she sagged and fell in a heap on the floor. "My goodness! What's wrong?" he exclaimed. When she regained consciousness, she explained. "Oh, this has been the worst day! Our son received a terrible report card; Mother was admitted to the hospital; the roast burned; the washing machine broke. Now to top it off, you come home drunk!"[2]

---

[2] Illustration from Building Your Mate's Self-Esteem by Dennis and Barbara Rainey (San Bernardino, Calif.: Here's Life Publishers, 1986).

If your partner can't even fathom the possibility that you would bring her flowers or a gift (or some similar surprise), take the hint. It's time to work on honoring your mate!

His & Her Discussion Questions

- Would you be shocked if I brought you flowers or some other gift?
- What's the best surprise I ever gave you?
- What kind of thoughtful gesture would be enjoyable and honoring to you?
- Do you prefer being surprised in front of friends or in private?

Our Prayer

Lord, we confess that the hurly-burly pace of living often threatens to suffocate our relationship. Remind us to care for each other. Help us to encourage others who are struggling in their marriages. Amen.

12

ARE YOU JESUS?

Command them to do good, to be rich in good deeds, and to be generous and willing to share. (1 Timothy 6:18 NIV)

After their meeting ran late, five out of town salesmen hurried as fast as they could to catch their train. As they raced through the terminal, one inadvertently kicked over a slender table on which rested a basket of apples. It belonged to a ten year old blind boy who was selling apples to pay for his books and clothes for school. The salesmen clambered aboard the train, but one felt compassion for the boy. He asked his friends to call his wife and tell her he would be late getting home.

Then he jumped off the train and returned to where the boy was standing. As the salesman gathered up the apples scattered across the floor, he noticed that several were bruised or split. Reaching into his pocket, he said to the boy, "Here's twenty dollars for the apples we damaged. I hope we didn't spoil your day. God bless you." As he walked away, the boy called after him, "Are you Jesus?"[3]

We are most like Christ when we show compassion and generosity to others. Jesus said, "Whatever you did for one of the least of these brothers of mine, you did for me" (Matthew 25:40). We reflect His character whether we're helping someone less fortunate or giving our mate a back rub at the end of the day.

His & Her Discussion Questions

- How do our interactions with others reflect the character of Jesus?
- When was the last time we stopped to help another person in need?
- How do you feel when you show compassion to someone else?

Our Prayer

Lord, we ask that Your extravagant love would flow through us each day to touch those around us. Show us how to serve, to help, and to give without expecting anything in return. Amen.

---

[3] Illustration from The Signature of Jesus by Brennan Manning (Sisters, Ore.: Multnomah Books, 1992). Reprinted in Stories for a Man's Heart, comp. Al and Alice Gray (Sisters, Ore.: Multnomah Publishers, Inc., 1999).

13

DECISIONS, DECISIONS

The head of every man is Christ, and
the head of the woman is man, and the
head of Christ is God.
(1 Corinthians 11:3 NIV)

Among the most controversial Scriptures are those
relating to a wife's obligation to "submit" to a
husband's leadership? This principle offends many
women. Furthermore, it places power in the hands of
men who sometimes misuse it. And yet, there it is,
time and again: "The husband is head of the wife."
Those words can't be brushed aside by those who rely
on Scripture as their infallible guide. But what does
this "headship" really mean?[4]

The Bible makes it clear that the husband is to be
the leader in his home, yet he has no right to run
roughshod over the opinions and feelings of his
wife. He is to love her as Christ loved the church

---

[4] Tendencies of the single man from Sexual Suicide by George Gilder (New
York, N.Y.: Quadrangle/The New York Times Book Company. 1973).

(Ephesians 5:25) and to serve her unselfishly and compassionately. A man should include his wife in making mutually satisfying decisions, always working to incorporate her perspectives, and seeking compromise when possible. In situations where they simply cannot find common ground, Scripture gives the man the prerogative—and responsibility—to choose and lead. Yet in this case, he must be more sensitive and considerate than ever, bearing in mind that he will ultimately answer to God not only for his choices, but for his treatment of his wife.

His & Her Discussion Questions

- (husband) How would you rate my leadership as your husband?
- Does our decision-making process fit the biblical model? (wife)
- How do you feel about your role as "leader in the home"?
- (husband) Am I sensitive to your feelings regarding decisions?

Our Prayer

Heavenly Father, in Your divine plan for marriage You have asked the husband to lead and the wife to submit, and we want so much to obey You. We come humbly now, asking for Your wisdom and help to do so. Amen.

14

ON TARGET

Get a new heart and a new spirit.
(Ezekiel 18:31 NIV)

Maybe you heard the story about the day Lisa finally had enough. Her husband, Greg, loved to shoot. An expert marksman, he traveled widely to compete against other enthusiasts, and occasionally he brought home a trophy. But Lisa had no interest in marksmanship. In fact, she didn't like guns—period. To make matters worse, she missed her husband terribly while he was away pursuing his hobby.

One day it dawned on her that their relationship was in trouble. That was the day Lisa finally had enough. Lisa asked Greg to teach her how to shoot a rifle, then joined him in his travels. Soon she decided to compete at the shooting events. To Lisa's surprise, she liked firing a rifle. And to her husband's surprise, Lisa was a very good shot. She even started bringing home more trophies than he did. But of the prizes they brought home, one stood out above all the rest: Their marriage seemed reborn. The time they spent together at their newfound common interest helped them develop a closeness that simply hadn't existed before.

Lisa's story is a good reminder that what seems like an obstacle might really be an opportunity. Creative, committed couples discover this secret every day. Just ask a husband who's learned to love ballroom dancing or a wife who's gotten hooked on fly fishing. That's because the best times always seem to come in pairs.

His & Her Discussion Questions

- When was the last time we tried a new activity together?
- Did you enjoy it? Why or why not?
- Are there activities keeping us apart that we could do together?

Our Prayer

Dear God, we ask for fresh determination to explore new interests and activities together. Where our marriage would be strengthened by playing together, help us let go of the old habits and assumptions that keep us apart. Amen.

15

GREAT GRACE

Consider the ravens: They do not sow or
reap . . . yet God feeds them. And how
much more valuable you are than birds!
(Luke 12:24 NIV)

Although the battle for healthy self confidence is
most often fought by women, many men also
struggle with the issue. Unlike a woman, a man derives
his sense of worth primarily from the reputation he
earns in his job or profession. He draws emotional satisfaction from achieving in business, becoming financially independent, developing a highly respected
skill, being the "boss," or being loved and appreciated
by his patients, clients, or business associates. When
his career fails, however, look out.

His confidence often falters, and he becomes
vulnerable. Depression, anger, and withdrawal are
just some of his potential responses. Wives, here's
something to remember: More than anything, your
man needs your respect. Compliment him on the

qualities you most admire in him. Avoid comments that debase or embarrass him—especially in the eyes of others. As much as is reasonably possible, understand and support his career, but also create such an affirming atmosphere at home that he will be happy to leave career concerns at the office.

The better you understand your differences, the more you'll appreciate the gift that is your mate.

His & Her Discussion Questions

- (wife) What achievement are you proudest of?
- (wife) Are you satisfied with the current state of your career?
- (wife) How can I help you with your career?
- (wife) How can I show more respect for you and what you do?

Our Prayer

(wife) Father, thank You for my husband—for the energy, skills, and ambitions you've placed in him. Help him to know that You love him no matter how he performs, and please help me show him the honor and respect I feel. Amen.

16

BODY & SPIRIT

Don't be afraid; you are worth more
than many sparrows.
(Matthew 10:31 NIV)

In addition to society's obsession with physical
beauty, women face other obstacles to maintaining confidence, including dis-respect for wives and
mothers who have chosen the traditional homemaking role. Furthermore, many wives, especially mothers of small children, feel isolated at home. Their
husbands are physically and emotionally "elsewhere,"
pursuing careers, hobbies, or both. The result is often
devastating, as women tend to derive their sense of
self worth from the emotional closeness achieved
through relationships.

What's the solution? We encourage you as the
husband to be present with your wife in body
and spirit. Set aside time for her. Listen to her.
Romance her. Show her she's still your one-and-only
sweetheart. On the other hand, don't expect to fill

all her emotional needs. Encourage her to develop meaningful friendships with other women and reach out to others in your community.

"Honor one another above yourselves." This simple phrase from the Bible (Romans 12:10 NIV) is the key to affirming the infinite worth of your spouse.

His & Her Discussion Questions

- (husband) When you're with other people, do you sometimes think, they wouldn't like me if they really knew who I am?
- (husband) Do you feel that I'm "present with you," or do I often seem preoccupied?
- (husband) What can I do to build your confidence this week?
- (husband) How can I support you in establishing friendships?

Our Prayer

(husband) Dear God, thank You for the great worth You see in my wife. I see it, too, and I want to honor and cherish her more every day. Help me to bless her and make her strong in this way. Amen.

17

DIVINE DECREE

> *God demonstrates his own love for us in this: While we were still sinners, Christ died for us.* (Romans 5:8 NIV)

We've talked about the powerful influence others have on the way we see ourselves. Yet we should always remember that true value is granted by the One who created us in the first place. There is no greater sense of self-worth than knowing that He is acquainted with me personally; that He values me more than the possessions of the entire world; that He understands my fears and anxieties; that He reaches out to me when no one else cares; that He can turn my liabilities into assets and my emptiness into fullness; and that He has a place prepared for me—one where earthly pain and suffering will be but a dim memory.

Indeed, the Lord of the universe places so much value on us that He gave His life to save us. What a fantastic message of hope and encouragement for those who are broken and discouraged! This is self worth at its richest—dependent not on the whims of birth or physical attractiveness or social judgment, but on the decree of our loving Lord.

His & Her Discussion Questions

- Do we base our self-image on the Lord's divine decree?
- What is it that really makes you feel valuable?
- Do I let you know often enough how much I value you?
- How can I better show how much I appreciate you?
- How can we remember that our worth as human beings is determined not by what we do or how we look or what we own, but by the fact that we are children of God?

Our Prayer

Lord, we want so much to view ourselves and others from an eternal perspective. May we build our lives together on Your grand scheme, not on what is temporary and insignificant. Help us to live each day by the truth of Your divine decree. Amen.

18

COST OF BITTERNESS

I tell you, {forgive} not seven times, but seventy-seven times.
(Matthew 18:22 NIV)

Just as we must act on Scripture's instruction to forgive, we should also consider the great cost of failing to do so. With-holding forgiveness brings on bitterness, which Neal T. Anderson says is like "battery acid in the soul." It leads to anger, resentment, depression, health problems, isolation, struggles with addictions, and more. It continues to haunt the person until he or she comes to terms with it. People who hang on to bitterness cause more pain to themselves than to the targets of their wrath.

A second cost is equally distressing. Jesus told a parable of an unmerciful servant who, after his master forgave him a large debt, demanded payment of a small debt from another servant. The master had the first servant thrown into jail and tortured. *This is how my heavenly Father will treat each of you,* Jesus said, *unless you forgive your brother from your heart* (Matthew 18:35 NIV).

For couples who want to follow God's way for marriage and who hope for His best in their relationship, forgiveness is not just a suggestion. It is a spiritual commandment!

His & Hers Discussion Questions

- Why is failing to forgive more damaging to us than to the one who wronged us?
- Are either of us bitter about something today? Why?
- What steps of forgiveness can we take together?
- How can we avoid bitterness in the future?

Our Prayers

Dear Lord, You have spoken plainly about the consequences of withholding forgiveness. Help us to hear You and obey. May we please You and bless each other with our quickness to forgive at all times. Amen.

19

HIT THE JACKPOT

*It is easier for a camel to go through the
eye of a needle than for a rich man to
enter the kingdom of God.*
(Matthew 19:24 NIV)

Do you ever dream of winning the lottery? It may
interest you to know that about a third of all
lottery winners go bankrupt within five years and
that another quarter of these instant millionaires
wind up selling their remaining payments at a dis-
counted rate to pay off debts. People who are reckless with ordinary paychecks are just as reckless with
bigger ones.

Rather than fantasize about hitting the jackpot, we
should strive to be better stewards of what we have.
Handle credit cards—if you must use them at all—
with great care and do everything you can to stay
out of debt, one of the foremost marriage destroyers.
Make purchases with cash when possible. Establish a
family budget and stick to it.

Remember to give at least 10 percent of your earnings to the Lord—after all, everything is His, anyway.

Above all, make sure you spend less than you earn each month. It takes discipline, but this simple formula will go a long way toward establishing a worry-free atmosphere in your home.

His & Her Discussion Questions

- Most people around the world would consider the average American income a jackpot. Do you?
- Are we saving money instead of falling into debt?
- Would we benefit from establishing a family budget or revising the one we have?
- Are we tithing?

Our Prayer

Heavenly Father, You bless us with so much. Even when money is tight, we know You care for us. But we often fail to be responsible and to honor You with how we manage money. Help us to know and live by Your wisdom. Amen

20

STRENGTH TO FORGIVE

If you hold anything against anyone, forgive him, so that your Father in heaven may forgive you your sins. (Mark 11:25 NIV)

Forgiveness is never easy, but it's the vital first step toward healing. A woman once wrote to tell "Dear Abby" that her husband of two years had had an affair with a young widow, who then carried his child. The wife wanted to die; she also wanted to kill her husband and the widow. But she knew those weren't the answers she needed. Instead, she prayed to God, and the Lord gave her the strength to forgive both the husband and the widow.

The baby was born in the home of the husband and wife and raised as their own. He turned out to be their only child. In fifty years, wife and husband never discussed the incident again. "But," the wife wrote, "I've read the love and gratitude in his eyes a thousand times."[5]

---

[5] "Dear Abby" illustration from The Christ-Centered Marriage by Neil T. Anderson and Charles Mylander (Ventura, Calif.: Gospel Light/Regal Books, 1996).

By praying for God's help, this woman received peace, a loving marriage, and a child she otherwise wouldn't have had. The next time anger and resentment rise in your throat, get on your knees, and ask the Lord for the healing work He wants to do in your heart. We believe He will hear and answer that prayer.

His & Her Discussion Questions

- Who in your life has been most difficult to forgive? Why?
- Is there someone you have never forgiven?
- How has God honored the times you've forgiven someone?
- Do we have anything that calls for forgiveness between us? What?
- How will forgiving now make our marriage stronger in the future?

Our Prayer

Dear Lord Jesus, forgiveness sometimes costs so much and hurts even more! But You forgave us—and now You ask us to forgive others. Teach us the healing power of forgiveness. Help us to bring this gift of love to our marriage again and again. Amen.

21

DOING WHAT COMES NATURAL

*Surely, I was sinful at birth, sinful from
the time my mother conceived me.*
(Psalm 51:5 NIV)

Humanistic and Christian psychologists differ
significantly in how they view human nature.
Secular psychologists see children as born "good,"
or at least "morally neutral." They believe children
learn to do wrong from parental mistakes and a cor-
rupt society.

As Christians, however, we know otherwise. Deep
within our character is a self will that is inborn, part
of our genetic nature. We desire to control people,
our circumstances, our environment—we want
what we want, and we want it now. Adam and Eve
demonstrated this when they ate the forbidden fruit.
Toddlers stomp their little feet and throw temper
tantrums. Husbands and wives illustrate the same
willfulness when they argue about how to spend
money—or about whether the toilet paper should

roll from the front or the back. King David referred to this basic human nature when he wrote, "In sin did my mother conceive me."

Only Jesus Christ can help us deal with the depravity that leads us to be selfish, arrogant, and disobedient. He has promised to do for us what we are powerless to accomplish on our own. Let's talk about that.

His & Her Discussion Questions

- Do you agree that humans are born with a bent toward sin? Why or why not?
- Is there an area of your life that used to be a struggle, but that you've given over to God with positive results?
- Do you think selfishness is a problem in our marriage?
- How can we encourage each other in this area?

Our Prayer

Father, we admit our sinful and selfish ways. We look to You for forgiveness and healing. Thank You for Your mercies. We need Your power to change— and we reach for it together. Amen.

Day 22

GREATEST GIFT

Consider the ravens: They do not sow or reap . . . yet God feeds them. And how much more valuable you are than birds!
(Luke 12:24 NIV)

Although the battle for healthy self confidence is most often fought by women, many men also struggle with the issue. Unlike a woman, a man derives his sense of worth primarily from the reputation he earns in his job or profession. He draws emotional satisfaction from achieving in business, becoming financially independent, developing a highly respected skill, being the "boss," or being loved and appreciated by his patients, clients, or business associates. When his career fails, however, look out.

His confidence often falters, and he becomes vulnerable. Depression, anger, and withdrawal are just some of his potential responses. Wives, here's something to remember: More than anything, your man needs your respect. Compliment him on the qualities you most admire in him. Avoid comments that debase or embarrass him—especially in the eyes of others. As much as is reasonably possible, understand and support his career, but also create such an affirming atmosphere at home that he will be happy to leave career concerns at the office.

The better you understand your differences, the more you'll appreciate the gift that is your mate.

His & Her Discussion Questions

- (wife) What achievement are you proudest of? (wife)
- Are you satisfied with the current state of your career?
- (wife) How can I help you with your career?
- (wife) How can I show more respect for you and what you do?

Our Prayer

(wife) Father, thank You for my husband—for the energy, skills, and ambitions you've placed in him. Help him to know that You love him no matter how he performs, and please help me show him the honor and respect I feel. Amen.

Day 23

RENEGADE MEN

---

*Fathers do not exasperate your children;
instead, bring them up in the training
and instruction of the Lord.*
(Ephesians 6:4 NIV)

Author Derek Prince has described the "renegade men" as one of society's biggest problems. The word renegade means "one who has shirked his primary responsibilities." It is an accurate description of those husbands and fathers who pour every resource into work or pleasure, leaving the child-rearing task entirely to their wives. Both boys and girls desperately need their fathers, who have a specific role to play in their lives.

Research in the field of child development has confirmed that the absence of positive masculine influence plays a key role in adolescent rebellion, sex-role identity, and cohesion within the family. Conversely, those who accept their God-given responsibilities at home have a fleeting—and golden—opportunity to shape the little lives entrusted to their care.

His & Her Discussion Questions

- (husband) Do I ever resemble a renegade male? How?
- (husband) In what ways have I been a good father? (For couples without children: What kind of father would I be?)
- (wife) How have our own fathers been good or poor examples of fulfilling their responsibilities at home?
- (wife) How, as a wife, can I help you be a better father?

Our Prayer

(husband) Dear God, thank You for the responsibility and opportunity to impact my children for good. I want to be faithful. Help me to celebrate— not resent—my fatherly duties. Through my sometimes-inadequate efforts, accomplish great things in the lives of my kids. Amen.

Day 24

OH, THE TROUBLES

'I hate divorce,' says the Lord God of Israel.
(Malachi 2:16 NLT)

Who would know better than the architect of marriage that living with another person day in and day out isn't always easy? God understands what we're going through, even in our worst circumstances. When Paul stated that *those who marry will face many troubles in this life* (1 Corinthians 7:28 NIV), he wasn't kidding! Fortunately, God has given us a blueprint in Scripture for success and fulfillment in our marriage relationship. The Lord designed marriage for our benefit, and He knows that destroying this partnership is harmful to us in countless ways.

No wonder God hates divorce. He has made it clear that the concept of separating permanently from one's marriage partner is not only unacceptable, but abhorrent. The only exception He has recorded for us is in the case of adultery, and even in that situation there is room for forgiveness and reconciliation if we follow Christ's merciful example.

Our encouragement to you as a husband and wife who seek God's best is a very personal one. As Brian and I have sought out and followed the Word of God, we have found all the stability and fulfillment in our marriage that He has promised! And you will, too. Marriage is His idea, after all, and His principles and values naturally produce harmony between people. Its sinful behaviors that kill a relationship.

When your time of "many troubles" strikes, Satan will be ready at just the right moment to suggest the "solution" of divorce. Perhaps you've already arrived at this place in the past. Surely you know and love couples who have come to this moment and have chosen to believe Satan's lie.

His & Her Discussion Questions

- No! We believe it is through the grace of our Lord Jesus that we are saved, just as they are. (Acts 15:11 **NIV**)
- Can we agree that divorce is not an option for us?
- Can we agree that no matter what storms or trouble come, that God will be the final authority in our marriage?

Our Prayer

Dear Lord, our prayer is that we believe and trust you with our marriage. We know that with your amazing grace we can and will stay together. Thank you for giving us your grace (supernatural power) to stand and stand together.

Day 25

THE BOTTOM LINE

Start children off on the way they should go, and even when they are old, they will not turn from it. (Proverbs 22:6 NIV)

The contradictory advice given in popular culture about what children need is enough to drive a conscientious parent to distraction. In days past, moms and dads learned child-rearing from their parents, who learned from theirs. Rightly or wrongly, they had a sense of confidence about what they were doing. That's because the traditional approach to parenting boils down to some very basic ideas.

Here are just a few:

—When your children ask, "Who's in charge?" tell them.

—When they mutter, "Who loves me?" take them in your arms and surround them with affection.

—When they defiantly challenge you, win decisively. Talk to them. Set up clear boundaries and then enforce the rules firmly and fairly.

—Expose your children to interesting things. Help them use their time wisely.

—Raise them in a stable family with two parents who love each other and enjoy a strong marriage.

—Teach them to love the Lord and understand His Word.

—Treat them with respect and dignity and expect the same in return.

—Set aside time to build friendship and love between generations. Then enjoy the sweet benefits of competent parenthood and a wonderful family!

His & Her Discussion Questions

- How are we doing on this list of parenting basics?
- Where do we see progress?
- Which ones need special attention?

Our Prayer

Father, thank You for the timeless wisdom that we can follow to help us raise our children right. May we parent wisely and lovingly, trusting in Your blessing. Amen.

Day 26

AN OPPOSITE COUPLE

"We must obey God rather than men!"
Acts 5:29

B rian and I describe ourselves as the "An Opposite Couple"—and it may be true. Brian says the only things they have in common are the same wedding anniversary and the same children. I'm more tell everything; he's more tell nothing. I enjoy Top 40 music; he prefers Hip-Hop at maximum volume. I grew up in a more heathen family; he grew up in a church family. And so it goes. Perhaps in part because of our differences, we have experienced nearly every imaginable conflict in marriage— over scheduling, communication, home life, finances, discipline of the children, and more. In over twenty years of marriage, however, we have learned to appreciate their differences. We have faced, and weathered, our fair share of storms. The key, is nothing fancy—simply obedience to the Lord. If there's hope for the An Opposite Couple, there's hope for the rest of you, too.

His & Her Discussion Questions

- Were you attracted by my "opposite" traits when we were dating?
- Have we survived despite our differences, or because of them?
- Do we accept the uniqueness of each other as God designed us, or do we struggle to "redesign" each other in our own images?
- Which of my traits that are different from yours do you appreciate most?

Our Prayer

Heavenly Lord, thank You for the differences that You weave together to make our marriage strong. Help us to respect, appreciate, and affirm these unique qualities more each day. Amen.

Day 27

LOVE AT FIRST SIGHT

For love is of God.
(1 John 4:7 KJV)

Some people believe that true love can occur the moment a man and woman lay eyes on each other. But "love at first sight" is a physical and emotional impossibility because you cannot love someone you don't even know. You have simply been drawn to the package in which they live.

A lifelong emotional attachment is much more than a romantic feeling. It is more than a sexual attraction or the thrill of the chase or a desire to get married. Such feelings usually indicate infatuation and tend to be temporary and rather selfish in nature. A person may say, "I can't believe what is happening to me. This is the most fantastic thing I've ever experienced! I must be in love." Notice that those who make these statements are not talking about the other person—they're excited about their own gratification. Such individuals haven't fallen in love with someone else; they've fallen in love with love.

Genuine love is not something one "falls" into, as though he or she was tumbling into a ditch. One cannot love an unknown object, regard-less of how beautiful or handsome it is. Only when a person begins to develop a deep appreciation and admiration for another—an intense awareness of his or her needs, strength, and character—has one begun to experience true love. From there, it should grow for a lifetime.

His & Her Discussion Questions

- Do you remember thinking that you were in love as a teenager, only to have that feeling fade over time?
- What did you think and feel when we first met?
- How did God show you that I should be your marriage partner?

Our Prayer

Dear Heavenly Father, thank You for the wonderful gift of love. Grant us your blessings, Father—more than we can even imagine right now! Amen.

Day 28

SPIRIT, HELP ME
BREAK OUT

*God did not give us a spirit of fear, but a
spirit of power, of love and of self-discipline.*
(2 Timothy 1:7 NKJV)

Breaking out of comfortable routines can be beneficial for us, but it isn't always as easy as it sounds. My grandfather, for example, hated automatic transmissions on automobiles because he had learned to drive with stick shifts. I've fallen into similar patterns. Until last year, I wrote books from notes in journals. And I had worked that way for years despite the availability of audio notes and transcribers. Now, all my writing is done via my Otter.ai App, boy is life much easier now!

Rigidity and the force of habit can cause us to do things that make no sense. Yet when we stop learning and growing, we fail to reach our potential. To look at it another way, which companies would you say are more successful in today's fast changing marketplace: those whose motto is "We've always done it this way," or those that continually evaluate their methods and seek improvements?

Some of what succeeds in business also makes sense in marriage. You might ask yourself if any outdated routines and pointless—or even costly—habits are holding you back.

His & Her Discussion Questions

- Am I stuck in any habits that no longer make sense?

- How are those who are unwilling to change like the Pharisees of Scripture? Consider the scriptures in Luke 11:37–44 NIV, *Your eye is the lamp of your body. When your eyes are healthy, your whole body also is full of light. But when they are unhealthy, your body also is full of darkness. See to it, then, that the light within you is not dark- ness. Therefore, if your whole body is full of light, and no part of it dark, it will be just as full of light as when a lamp shines its light on you.*

- Do you enjoy learning?

- How can I encourage you to get out of old ruts or discard outdated habits?

Our Prayer

Lord, we can become so comfortable in our old ways, but comfort can lead to stagnation and retreat. Inspire us by Your Spirit "of power, of love and of self-discipline" to reach for Your creative best. Thank You for the gift of new life we can enjoy together every day. Amen.

Day 29

TWO HOMES

If a house is divided against itself,
that house cannot stand.
(Mark 3:25 NIV)

Suppose that you're seven years old. You arrive home from school, and your mother welcomes you with a smile and a snack. Later your father comes home. Mom and Dad greet each other with a kiss and loving words. Dad gives you a warm hug. That night, after you finish your homework, the three of you enjoy a family game. Finally, you say your prayers and fall asleep.

Now put yourself in another seven year old's place. You come home from school to a mother who, when she's home at all, is on the phone or watching television. You eat a bag of candy by yourself. Later your father returns. Mom complains about the unfinished garage project. Dad replies angrily and walks past you to the kitchen. You watch television all evening, then crawl into bed and fall asleep listening to your parents argue.

One home is safe and nurturing: the other lonely and contentious. Too often, children grow up in homes like the latter—or worse. So, ask yourself: Which scenario best describes your family? Further, how would you describe the mood of your household? Divided or united? Amiable or argumentative? Supportive or sarcastic? Every day, the story of your home is etching itself into the spirit and memory of your children.

His & Her Discussion Questions

- How does the way we were brought up affect the mood in our household today?
- How do you think our children would describe our home?
- How can we make sure our home is a positive environment?

Our Prayer

Loving Lord, we know that our relationship sets the tone for our children's growing-up experience. Help us make our marriage the starting point of a good home and of a happy, Christ-honoring childhood for our kids. Amen.

Day 30

WANDERING SHEEP

If a man owns a hundred sheep, and one
of them wanders away, will he not leave
the ninety-nine . . . and go to look for the
one that wandered off?
(Matthew 18:12 NIV)

If you are parents of small children, you know exactly how the shepherds mentioned in the Bible felt as they watched over their flocks. Even for a mother with "eyes in the back of her head," keeping one active child from wandering off can seem as big a challenge as corralling a hundred sheep!

Jesus is called a shepherd, too, but His flock is all of humanity and He watches over us day and night. That's why He called Himself the Good Shepherd. He came to earth to die so that not one soul would have to be lost. During His earthly ministry, He was always on the lookout for lost souls. He stayed up late to talk to Nicodemus, He came to Jesus at night and said, *Rabbi, we know that you are a teacher who has come from God. For no one could perform the signs you are doing if God were not with him.* (John 3:2 NIV). He wouldn't let Zacchaeus hide unnoticed in a tree *When Jesus reached the spot, he looked up and said to him, "Zacchaeus, come down immediately. I must stay at your house today."* (Luke 19:5 NIV). And when the Pharisees were about to stone a despised adulteress, Jesus intervened with a message of forgiveness and direction— *"Go, and sin no more"* (John 8:11 NIV).

Every day, we have divine appointments to lead others into God's flock—not just our family, friends, neighbors, and coworkers, but also people we've never met before and may never see again. God's wisdom and power are at our disposal. We must keep our eyes open.

His & Her Discussion Questions

- Do you see Jesus as your Good Shepherd? Why or why not?
- As a couple, are we watching for "lost sheep"?
- How can we be more watchful for opportunities to reach unbelievers?
- Is there anyone "lost" with whom we can talk this week?

Our Prayer

Lord Jesus, show us how to demonstrate Your great love and compassion to those around us. We, too, want to be shepherds of lost souls. Amen

Day 31

RIGHT MOTIVES

I belong to my beloved, and his desire is for me.
(Song of Songs 7:10 NIV)

Let's face it: Sex is a topic on the mind of just about every husband and wife. (Some wives claim their husbands think of nothing else!) The physical union of man and woman is one of the most pleasurable and meaningful aspects of marriage. Yet when a couple engages in sex for the wrong reasons, intercourse quickly loses its significance and can become an empty obligation. The late Dr. David Hernandez once offered some common, "non-loving" motives for sex:

- To fulfill one's marital duty,
- To repay or secure a favor,
- As a conquest,
- As a substitute for verbal communication,
- To overcome feelings of inferiority,
- As an enticement for emotional love,

- As a defense against anxiety and tension,
- As a form of self-gratification without seeking to satisfy the other.

God designed sex as an intimate expression of love between husband and wife. Anything that fails to meet that standard leaves one partner feeling unsatisfied and exploited.

His & Her Discussion Questions

- When was the last time you thought about making love?
- Does your motive for sex ever fall into any of the above categories?
- Have you ever felt sexually "used" by me?
- How can we move from "having sex" toward "making love"?

Our Prayer

Heavenly Father, You have blessed our union with sexual expression. Bless us with emotional and sexual intimacy as well. Thank You for the pleasure and wonder of married lovemaking. Amen.

SECTION 2

31 Ways to Simply Affirm

Affirm and you are affirmed

Today is a new day for you and your spouse. *This is the day which the Lord hath made; we will rejoice and be glad in it. (Psalms 118:24* KJV) Today is a day for you to begin creating a joyous, fulfilling life. *You make known to me the path of life; you will fill me with joy in your presence, with eternal pleasures at your right hand. (Psalms 16:11NIV)*

Today is the day to begin to release all your limitations. But Jesus looked at them and said, *With man this is impossible, but with God all things are possible. (Matthew 19:26 ESV)*

Today is the day for you to learn the secrets of life. *Making known to us the mystery of his will, according to his purpose, which he set forth in Christ. (Ephesians 1:9 ESV)*

You can change your life for the better. *The Lord will keep you from all harm— he will watch over your life; the Lord will watch over your coming and going both now and forevermore. (Psalms 121:7-8 ESV)*

You already have the tools within you to do so. These tools are your thoughts and your beliefs. *Do not conform to the pattern of this world, but be transformed by the renewing of your mind. Then you will be able to test and approve what God's will is—his good, pleasing and perfect will. (Romans 12:2 NIV)*

In this chapter, we will teach you how to use affirmations as a tool to improve the quality of your life and the lives around you.

What Are Positive affirmations?

For those of you who aren't familiar with the benefits of positive affirmations, I'd like to explain a little about them. An affirmation is really anything you say or think. It's a declaration. Often what we normally speak and think is quite negative and doesn't create good experiences for us. We must retrain our *thinking* and *speaking* into positive patterns if we want to change our lives. *A good man brings good things out of the good stored up in his heart, and an evil man brings evil things out of the evil stored up in his heart. For the mouth speaks what the heart is full of. (Luke 6:45 NIV).*

It seems like a common misconception that behaving well is sufficient to be a Christian, but the Bible says otherwise!! Our thoughts matter equally! The first and most important about transformational thinking is that it is inspired by God and commanded of us to do. It's required 'if' we want to be able to test and approve what God's will is – his good, pleasing, and perfect will. Is it not true? Stop and read *Romans 12:2* one more time and then let's proceed.

I believe this is such an important thing to teach and share, especially when helping people pray! It seems like a common misconception that behaving well is sufficient to being a Christian, but the Bible says otherwise!! Our thoughts matter equally! Affirmations are a great tool along with the Word of God in practice; to transforming your mind and those around you. Now, when I speak of those around you – I literally mean everyone around you. For the purpose pf this book, we are focusing on our spouse or family which is pivotal in who matters most to you.

I'd like to share these scriptures to give you a good list to begin with from the Word of God.

We demolish arguments and every pretension that sets itself up against the knowledge of God, and we take captive every thought to make it obedient to Christ. (2 Corinthians 10:5 NIV)

Whatever is true, whatever is honorable, whatever is just, whatever is pure, whatever is lovely, whatever is commendable, if there is any excellence, if there is anything worthy of praise, think about these things. (Philippians 4:8 ESV)

Set your minds on things that are above, not on things that are on earth. (Colossians 3:2 ESV)

For those who live according to the flesh set their minds on the things of the flesh, but those who live according to the Spirit set their minds on the things of the Spirit. For to set the mind on the flesh is death, but to set the mind on the Spirit is life and peace. (Romans 8:5-6 ESV)

Let all bitterness and wrath and anger and clamor and slander be put away from you, along with all malice. Be kind to one another, tenderhearted, forgiving one another, as God in Christ forgave you. (Ephesians 4:31-32 ESV)

May my meditation be pleasing to him, for I rejoice in the Lord. (Psalm 104:34 ESV)

Either make the tree good and its fruit good, or make the tree bad and its fruit bad, for the tree is known by its fruit. You brood of vipers! How can you speak good when you are evil? For out of the abundance of the heart the mouth speaks. The good person out of his good treasure brings forth good, and the evil person out of his evil treasure brings forth evil. I tell you, on the Day of Judgment people will give account for every careless word they speak, for by your words you will be justified, and by your words you will be condemned." *(Matthew 12:33-37 ESV)*

If then you have been raised with Christ, seek the things that are above, where Christ is, seated at the right hand of God. Set your minds on things that are above, not on things that are on earth. (Colossians 3:1-2 ESV)

And to be renewed in the spirit of your minds, (Ephesians 4:23 ESV)

Be sober-minded; be watchful. Your adversary the devil prowls around like a roaring lion, seeking someone to devour. (1 Peter 5:8 ESV)

The good person out of his good treasure brings forth good, and the evil person out of his evil treasure brings forth evil. I tell you, on the day of judgment people will give account for every careless word they speak, for by your words you will be justified, and by your words you will be condemned. (Matthew 12:35-37 ESV)

An affirmation opens the door. It's a beginning point on the path to change. In essence, you're saying to your subconscious mind: *"I am taking responsibility. I am aware that there is something I can do to change."* When I talk about *doing affirmations,* I mean consciously choosing words that will either help *eliminate* something from your life or help *create* something new in your life.

Every thought you think and every word you speak is an affirmation. All our self-talk, our internal dialogue, is a stream of affirmations. You're using affirmations every moment whether you know it or not. You're affirming and creating your life experiences with every word and thought. And you get to choose: Are you going to glorify God? Or are you going to align with the Enemy and criticize God's work and creation?

Your beliefs are merely habitual thinking patterns that you learned as a child or have been formed as you've grown into adulthood from environments, experiences, internal and external factors. Many of them work very well for you. Other beliefs may be limiting your ability to create the very life or marriage you say you want. What you want and what you believe you deserve may be very different. You need to pay attention to your thoughts so that you can begin to eliminate the ones manifesting or experiences you do *not* want in your life.

Please realize that every complaint is an affirmation of something you think you don't want in your life. Every time you get angry, you're affirming that you want more anger in your life. Every time you feel like a victim, you're affirming that you want to *continue* to feel like a victim. If you feel that life isn't giving you what you want in your world, then it's certain that you will never have the goodies that God kind of life gives to others-that is, until you change the way you think and talk. Consider this, when we stop sounding ungrateful and greedy, don't you think God will be able to be generous in your life?

It's time to learn *how* to think and talk. Our thoughts create our experiences. Your parents probably didn't know this, so they couldn't possibly teach it to you. They taught you how to look at life in the way that *their* parents taught them. It's time for all of us to wake up and begin to consciously shape our lives in a way that pleases and supports God. *You* can do it. *I* can do it. *We all* can do it-we just need to learn how and invite the Holy Spirit to guide us, teach us, and empower us. So, let's get to it.

Throughout this section, I'll talk about affirmations in general, and then we'll get to specific areas for yourself, your spouse, and your children if you have any. This is a small section, because once you learn how to use affirmations, then you can apply the principles in all situations. Some people say that "affirmations don't work" (which is an affirmation in itself), when what they mean is that they don't know how to use them correctly. They may say, *"My marriage is growing and thriving,"* but then think, *Oh, this is stupid, I know it won't work.* Which affirmation do you think will win out? The negative one, of course, because it's part of a long-standing, habitual way of looking at life. Sometimes people will say their affirmations once a day and complain the rest of the time. It will take a long time for affirmations to work if they're done that way. The complaining affirmations will always win, because there are more of them and they're usually said with great feeling.

However, *saying* affirmations is only part of the process. What you do the rest of the day and night is even more important. The secret to having your affirmations work quickly and consistently is to prepare an atmosphere for them to grow in. Affirmations are like seeds planted in soil. Poor soil, poor growth. Rich soil, abundant growth. The more you choose to think thoughts that honor God–the quicker the affirmations work.

So, think God thoughts- Good thoughts, it's that simple. And it *is* doable. The way you choose to think, right now, is just that — a choice. You may not realize it because you've thought this way for so long, but it really is a choice. Now... today... this moment... you can choose to change your thinking.

Your life won't turn around overnight, but if you're consistent and make the choice daily to think thoughts, you'll see positive changes in every area of your life. Now, I have to say this, often our own pleasure is rarely a God-honoring goal. The Bible says in (Hebrews 11:3 NIV) *By faith we understand that the worlds were framed by the word of God, so that the things which are seen were not made of things which are visible.* In that same way, you frame your world by the words you say.

The Bible expresses this also in (Proverbs 18:21 KJV), *Death and life are in the power of the tongue: and they that love it shall eat the fruit thereof.* It's important to speak fruit onto the tree that you'll be eating from. Now, it's time to get started putting these God Thoughts-Good Thoughts into practice. We'll begin with the husband affirming his wife, followed by the wife affirming her husband and end with both affirming the children.

The Importance of Husbands Speaking Words of Affirmation to Your Wives

It may feel complicated and confusing trying to understand your wife and her emotional needs, but daily affirmations will give her the smile you've been looking for. Don't worry, you have what it takes; affirmations are simply kind words you know to be true. Sincerely try these five affirmations with your wife and see how consistently speaking kindly to her will affect your marriage.

You are a blessing. Tell her out loud you are thankful for her add something special that you're thankful for here). It should be sincere to be effective. Gratitude is critical for great connection. This affirmation is especially great to say in the morning. When you declare her a blessing first thing, gratitude becomes the lens through which you see your relationship which can help prevent conflict.

You are beautiful. Her outward physical beauty is important to affirm. Never stop complimenting your wife's physical beauty. Some women with poor self-image try to sabotage their husband's affirmations but persist with your affirmation anyway. Inner beauty includes positive personality characteristics you find attractive. "I love the way you really care about people you interact with. You are beautiful inside and out."

You are loved. Sure, we overuse the word love for everything. "I love bacon, I love power tools, and I love Netflix." But declaring your love in a relationship *is* special. You may even remember the first time you told her you loved her. Even if you think she should already know, tell her she is loved every day.

You are desired. Every woman has a deep craving to be desirable. Pursue your wife in a way which demonstrates she is desired, and you will connect deeper than ever before. Remember that connecting deeper isn't always sexual, but it can be in wanting to spend time together doing small things like a movie, taking walk, or simply saying with words that you desire her more than just physically. Make it plain.

You are a great wife. Of all the relationships you have in your life, your marriage relationship is uniquely special. Affirm her success in your relationship. Tell her she is doing a great job of loving you. You could start by letting her know that you notice how she shows up for you in the small things that you appreciate like ensuring you have all your essentials (i.e., toothpaste, deodorant, shampoo), if you don't buy those things for yourself. You notice that she is a good at remembering to celebrate others or calls your mother when you forget. The wife sometimes fills in the gaps you may not even think of, spend a moment thinking of the ways she helps you help yourself without you asking her to do so. She will be glad you noticed AND affirmed her in doing so.

Each affirmation intentionally begins with the word *you*. The focus should be on encouraging *her*. When giving affirmations it is easy to start with yourself. "I'm blessed to be your husband" is nice, but the point of saying what is true about her can get lost when you start with *I*.

Side note: When you are having a difficult conversation or an argument, start with I. When tensions are high, starting with the word you will sound demeaning and accusatory. For example, "You always spend too much money." In a heated discussion begin by explaining how you feel in the situation. For example, "I feel overwhelmed at the thought of working more overtime when we overspend our budget."

To add emphasis to your positive affirmations pair them with affection. Saying '*I love you*' sounds even better when you are physically close to her. Communication works best when you use both words and actions.

Telling them is good, showing them is awesome, doing both is lifechanging. Don't settle for talk only. Words with no action is lying. Saying you love her but not acting in loving ways destroys trust. You become a conman, spewing sweet words, and never following through. Action with no words is confusing. Although it's awesome to have a spouse who consistently acts in loving ways, marriage can become awkward in silence. Like living with a mime who gets all the actions right, a marriage without verbal affirmation quickly becomes confusing and lonely. When you tell your spouse, she is beautiful and act in ways that make her feel beautiful, you will have a genuinely wonderful marriage.

The Importance of Wives Speaking Words of Affirmation to Your Husbands

When we were first married, I realized how my husband doesn't like to talk about his feelings. In fact, I felt he clammed up from the minute we said, "I do!" Sure, he still expressed his love to me and told me how much he cared, but he wasn't one to just open and talk about all his feelings. In fact, it's been a process over the twenty years we've been married to open more and more, little by little.

Being an extrovert by nature, that caught me off guard. Then, I found myself not sharing *my* heart with him as often and there became a gap of communication between us. I started to feel like I needed to reserve my own feelings, so I drew back. It's very true that not having regular and healthy communication with your spouse is dangerous. Also, be introspective because you may have been like me and needed to hear from your spouse or perhaps it could be something else causing you to draw back. Is this because his silence hurt you?

Did you withhold the way you showed love/your conversation because you were feeling hurt, spiteful, or bitter? Or was it that his lack of reciprocated conversation made you less eager to share your thoughts and feelings? Did you perceive his lack of sharing as disinterest? Was your withdrawal intentional/deliberate or unconscious?

How words of affirmation matter to men.

Men crave respect and knowing they are valued. Speaking words of affirmation into their lives, even if that's not their love language, helps them know how much we as wives care.

After a while, I quickly realized the error of my ways. In withholding my inner most thoughts and feelings, my new husband simply didn't feel validated or appreciated.

Simple words and daily reminders can help them feel respected and appreciated. This gives them the fuel and affirmation they need to take on the world each day. This simple token of appreciation will also strengthen the bond of your relationship.

Simple ways to share words of affirmation

Affirming your husband doesn't have to be long, mushy, or drawn-out conversations. In fact, some of the best ways we communicate aren't through conversations at all. I love to:

- Send him a sweet text during the day.
- Leave him a note by the coffee pot or even sneak one into his lunch.
- Do a simple act of service to show I care.
- Send him a sweet meme. (Facebook is good for something, right?!)
- Brag on him in front of other people.
- Leave a note on the bathroom mirror.

Words of Affirmation for Men

There is a big difference in the words of affirmation a woman longs to hear and what men crave to hear. Throughout the years, I realized I often shared the affirming words that *I* thought were important, and not the words that mattered most to him.

I recently asked my husband what words or phrases would help him feel loved and appreciated the most. While every man is different, here's some starting points as you learn to regularly speak words of affirmation into your husband.

- I respect you
- I appreciate you
- You're the best at ...

- You bless me because…
- I'm grateful for your hard work
- You're still my top choice
- I'm attracted to you
- I notice how hard you've been trying to…
- You make me laugh when…
- You're sexy when…
- Thank you for…
- You still have my heart
- I love it when you…
- Your opinion matters to me
- Thanks for talking about your feelings
- I appreciate your honesty
- When you help me with…I fall in love all over again
- You still make me melt
- I love the person you've become

Ladies don't let your husband's tough exterior get in the way of speaking life and encouraging words to him. Watch and see how this simple act will change your relationship.

The Importance of Parents Speaking Words of Affirmation to Your Children (if applicable)

Not many people will dispute the fact that it is important for parents to love, encourage, and support their kids so they will grow up as healthy and well-adjusted individuals. It is also important that children learn how to create these feelings within themselves. When children grow while learning how to create positive feelings and beliefs for themselves, it'll be much more difficult later in life for friends, family, and evil people to bring them down.

All children must deal with unfavorable situations at certain times in their lives. If they feel bad about the situation, it may cause them to become more negatively motivated. Words of affirmation are meant to help our children think more positively about negative situations and work towards focusing on the positive. For example,

How We Feel About Ourselves Is How We Develop

When people feel they are worthless, they start to behave like they are worthless. Believe it or not, it's important that as parents we give our children opportunity to contribute to the family good. Rather than just sharing great remarks with no effort on the child's part. Create ways that children can participate, and you can encourage with good words. By the same token, when people think they are special and loved by many, they will behave like they are loved and special. Although, we must be careful not to bring up children who feel entitled It's very easy to puff up our children or make statements that *we* think are helpful but are not. For example, telling kids "You're smart" *seems* nice, but what are you *saying*? You're observant, you learned that quickly, you have a good memory, you're hard-working, you're persistent, you're diligent, etc. Therefore, it is important for parents to offer encouraging words of affirmation to their children as they grow to help them build a personal positive foundation in which to build on in the future. This is truly about maintaining a good Godly balance within our homes and family structures. Once a child has a positive foundation, it'll be more difficult for those foundations to be torn down by others. We must remember that for our children we want their foundations built on solid rocks and not shifting sands. Their foundation must be in Jesus

Christ first and to build them up so how other people think about them isn't unbalanced or a greater focus.

Affirmations can be given to our children at any point during the day. From when they wake up in the morning to when they go to sleep at night, small affirmations can be given to help them foster a positive self-image. Even when you are strapping them into their toddler car seat, you can take the time to give them a little boost in confidence. Some kids get stressed when strapped into their toddler car seat and will need you to reassure them and teach them there is nothing to be afraid of. I want to share with you 25 good affirmations for children of all ages, young and old. But before I get into these thoughts and affirmations, I want to share this with you too. When I'm feeling cranky or annoyed (especially at my children), and I start wanting to grumble, complain, or criticize, I switch over to telling them how much God loves them and how He has special work and experiences just for them. Telling them who they are to God helps me to shift my focus because it reminds me that these children don't belong to me, they belong to God and I am a steward with the privilege and trust that I will nurture and not abuse His creation. When I feel angry, telling my children who they are to God helps remind me that I answer to God for the way I speak to them.

For example, I have turned "You're a real piece of work" as a sarcastic statement to a positive affirmation, "You are God's handiwork. He made you in His image, and He knew you and loved you before anyone else even knew you existed. You are His precious creation, and He has so many wonderful experiences in store for you. But, my love, it is important that you learn to obey me in the small things so that you will have practice to obey Him in the big things so that you will be able to experience all of the good things He has planned for you." I hope that you catch my drift here.

Here are 25 affirmations for children, young and old:

1. There is no one better to be than yourself.
2. You are enough.
3. You get better every single day.
4. You are an amazing person.
5. You are beautiful or handsome.
6. You are a leader.
7. You are creative.
8. Your challenges help you grow.
9. You are great just the way you are.
10. Your mistakes help you learn and grow.
11. Today is going to be a great day.
12. You have courage and confidence.

13. I can control my own happiness.

14. You have people who love and value you.

15. Believe in yourself. We believe in you.

16. Believe in your goals and dreams.

17. It's okay not to know everything.

18. Today, you can choose to think positive.

19. You can get through anything.

20. You can do anything you put my mind to.

21. You can make good choices.

22. You will do better next time.

23. You have everything in you to succeed.

24. You are capable of so much.

25. Set the tone and be the example.

We say this to our children all the time and each one of them has taken on being good stewards of themselves. Although not your typical affirmation, it's a way for them to think of themselves and have the confidence of every other affirmation we speak over them. This is to be said and shared freely and lovingly.

Why Be Kind to Ourselves?

Affirmations provide children with the ability to learn to truly look at themselves and provide themselves with positive affirmations when needed. However,

I think it's important that these be based on bibli-cal truth and not just ego-inflation. This leads us to another benefit a positive affirmation. People need to learn how to give themselves positive self-talk and treat themselves kindly. As we grow, it can be easy to speak to ourselves with criticism. This is harmful to our self-confidence and self-esteem. It can also lower our ability to be resilient to outside factors. When we model for our children positive self-talk from a young age, it'll help prevent them from learning self-criticism and remain strong because they have already created a positive belief system within them-selves. So, keep in mind that the way we as parents speak about ourselves will be observed and imitated by our children? For example, moms who are con-stantly criticizing the way they look, "Ugh, my hair looks awful," "Ugh, these pants make me look so fat," "Ugh, these bags under my eyes" etc. train girls to be critical of themselves. Be on guard to avoid this. It'll help your children in the long run. You've heard the saying, 'more is caught than taught'.

Affirmations Help against Bullying

Bullying is a huge issue many children face around the world. To deal with situations with bullies, self-confidence is key. Positive affirmations help our kids keep a positive mind in bullying scenarios, so they are not torn down. When children have been helped to develop a positive mental pathway, they can be more resilient after bullying situations and be able to cope and safeguard their self-esteem.

Consider this, a counterargument might be that false bravado invites bullying. We still must share and speak to our children that Jesus teaches about how to treat people who wrong us, and, more importantly, to trust in the Lord to take up our cause, and to trust that even though it may seem like people are getting away with sinning, God sees everything, and He judges justly.

Positive Affirmations to Speak to Your Children

1. I'm so thankful God chose to put you in our family.
2. Your sense of humor is something that I love.
3. My favorite job is being your mom.
4. Nothing you ever do will make me stop loving you.
5. You make me feel proud.
6. I smile when I look at you.
7. There is no one in the world who is like you, and that is wonderful.
8. If I could choose out of all the kids in the world, I would choose YOU.
9. Jesus loves you.

10. I am so proud of you.

11. You are such a diligent worker.

12. That was a very wise choice.

13. I believe in you.

14. You make me laugh.

15. Your siblings are so blessed to have you.

16. I'm listening.

17. That was really kind of you to do that.

18. The day you were born was one of the best days of my life.

19. You have such great ideas!

20. Spending time with you is one of my favorite things to do.

21. I love to see how you are growing up.

22. You are so special.

23. I think you are awesome!

24. I appreciate you so much.

25. Being around you is so fun.

This is the absolute list that <u>must</u> be shared for some reason every week.

Everything on this list. Without fail. I promise you; no, I guarantee you- that the children this is spoken to will be forever changed. Test it. And email us and tell us how you've seen your child change in attitude, behavior, responses, and communications with you. This is a guaranteed game changer for your household. There are 6 things. Six represents the number of man and speaking these six things to your child at least once per week will change the man or woman they will grow to become.

1. I love you (Say this to them out loud and often).
2. I'm proud of you. (Find something they did or said).
3. I'm sorry. (Parents sometimes speak out of fear or anger). There may be a reason you need to say this and it's okay to do so when warranted.
4. I forgive you. (Children sometimes say or do things that anger or frustrate us). We can forgive which in turn will teach them to forgive when warranted.
5. I'm listening.
6. You've got what it takes.

Now, we believe it is important to add scripture to what we speak and share with our children. Here is a list of examples in the scripture to rightly affirm with the blood of Jesus.

Godly Affirmations to teach Children to Speak over Themselves

"I am a Child of God."
Yet to all who did receive him, to those who believed in his name, he gave the right to become children of God—(John 1:12 NIV)

"God knitted me together inside my Mommy's tummy."
For You created my inmost being you knit me together in my mother's womb. (Psalm 139:13 NIV)

"God sings love songs over me."
The Lord your God is with you, the Mighty Warrior who saves. He will take great delight in you; in his love he will no longer rebuke you but will rejoice over you with singing. (Zephaniah 3:17 NIV)

"God created me to look just like Him."
So, God created mankind in his own image, in the image of God he created them; male and female he created them. (Genesis 1:27 NIV)

"I belong to God"
But now, this is what the LORD says-- he who created you, O Jacob, he who formed you, O Israel: "Fear not, for I have redeemed you; I have summoned you by name; you are mine. (Isaiah 43:1 NIV)

"I am Loved and Chosen"
For he chose us in him before the creation of the world to be holy and blameless in his sight. (Ephesians 1:4 NIV)

"I am God's Masterpiece"
For we are God's masterpiece. He has created us anew in Christ Jesus, so we can do the good things he planned for us long ago. (Ephesians 2:10 NLT)

"My name is written on God's hand"
See, I have engraved you on the palms of my hands; your walls are ever before me. (Isaiah 49:16 NIV)

"God is always with me"
Do not fear, for I am with you; do not be dismayed, for I am your God. I will strengthen you and help you.
I will uphold you with my righteous right hand. (Isaiah 41:10 NIV)

"God thinks about me all the time"
How precious to me are Your thoughts, God! How vast is the sum of them! Were I to count them, they would outnumber the grains of sand, when I awake, I am still with You. (Psalm 139:17-18 NIV)

"God takes good care of me"

Look at the birds of the air; they do not sow or reap or store away in barns, and yet your heavenly Father feeds them. Are you not much more valuable than they? (Matthew 6:26 NIV)

"God is for me, I will not fear"

The Lord is with me; I will not be afraid.
What can mere mortals do to me? (Psalm 118:6 NIV)

"God hears me when I cry"

In my distress I called to the LORD; I cried to my God for help. From his temple he heard my voice; my cry came before Him, into His ears. (Psalm 18:6 NIV)

"I can do all things because Jesus makes me strong"

For I can do all things through Christ, who gives me strength. (Philippians 4:13 NLT)

"God has good plans for me"

For I know the plans I have for you," declares the LORD, "plans to prosper you and not to harm you, plans to give you hope and a future. (Jeremiah 29:11 NIV)

"God watches over me when I sleep"

When you lie down, you will not be afraid; when you lie down, your sleep will be sweet. (Proverbs 3:24 NIV)

"I am Strong and Courageous"

Have I not commanded you? Be strong and courageous. Do not be afraid; do not be discouraged, for the LORD your God will be with you wherever you go.
(Joshua 1:9 NIV)

"God's Angels watch over me"

For He will command His angels concerning you to guard you in all your ways; they will lift you up in their hands, so that you will not strike your foot against a stone. (Psalm 91:11-12 NIV)

SECTION 3

31+ Ways to Simply Affirm

Of Targeted Prayers for Everything (or at least a few) Things that May Concern You

---

8 Ways Develop a More Powerful Prayer Life

Here are eight ways that have helped me develop a more powerful prayer life. I hope they will encourage you to.

1. Know to whom you are speaking.

Prayer is a conversation with God, and every conversation begins by addressing the person to whom you are speaking by name. Jesus begins with "Our Father in heaven." He focuses on a distinct person—the Heavenly Father with whom he has a personal relationship. We share the same right to call

God "Father," and there are times when we need to talk with our Abba Father, Daddy God. But God is three distinct persons in One: the Father, the Son, and the Holy Spirit.

2. Thank Him. I thank God in every prayer I pray.

A heartfelt thank you is always a great conversation starter. Like any parent, God loves to see that we have grateful hearts. But more importantly, as we take the time to praise God for all He has done in the past—the answered prayers, the impossible situations overcome, the healings and grace—our faith to believe for even greater answers to prayer grows stronger and more confident. Praise opens the gates of heaven and should always be part of our alone time with God.

3. Ask for God's will.

The Lord's Prayer is not the only place where Jesus modeled a heart of obedience and submission to the will of God over his own desires and needs. In the Garden of Gethsemane, only hours before Jesus' crucifixion, he prayed, "not my will, but yours be done." In a world where right and wrong are frequently confused and the future is so uncertain, it can be hard to know how to pray or what to ask for when difficult circumstances arise. But the one thing we can know with absolute certainty is that God's plan for those who love Him is good, and the safest place we can be is in the center of his divine will.

4. Ask God for wisdom and discernment to recognize His will.

Many people are frustrated because they don't "hear" from God, but if they would faithfully read His Word and know who He is, He would give them the guidance they're seeking without having to be audible. *If any of you lacks wisdom, you should ask God, who gives generously to all without finding fault, and it will be given to you.* (James 1:5 NIV)

5. Say what you need.

In Jesus' time, bread was a staple—one of the most basic needs of life—and he did not hesitate to ask God to provide it. But we often hesitate to come to God with the little things we need, thinking he shouldn't be bothered. And when the big problems come, we try everything we can to solve the problem before we think to pray. The Bible says in (James 4:2b NIV), *"You do not have because you do not ask God."* So, you never have to hesitate to ask God for what you need. Your Father in heaven delights to give you good gifts. The Bible speaks clearly in (Matthew 7:9-11 NIV) *"Which of you, if your son asks for bread, will give him a stone? Or if he asks for a fish, will give him a snake? If you, then, though you are evil, know how to*

give good gifts to your children, how much more will your
Father in heaven give good gifts to those who ask him!"

6. Ask for forgiveness.

James 5:16 **NIV** reads *"Confess your faults one to*
another, and pray one for another, that ye may be healed.
The effectual fervent prayer of a righteous man availeth
much." It reminds us that if we want our prayers to be
heard, our hearts need to be right with God and with
one another. If you feel your prayers are bouncing off
the ceiling, take some time to check your heart and
obey the command.

7. *Pray with a friend.*

There is power in agreement when we pray in Jesus'
name. When I have an urgent need to take before the
throne of God, I will often call a friend to pray with
me. If you don't already have one, make finding a
trusted prayer partner one of your goals. We just read
the fervent effectual prayer of the righteous availeth
much in James 5:16. This can be a friend who prays
with us.

8. *Pray the Word.*

My mother was a spiritual prayer warrior/intercessor,
and much that I know about prayer I learned from
her. I loved to listen to her pray because for every
need or situation, she would claim a scripture of

promise. "The Word of God has power and is our great spiritual weapon," My mother would say. "Pray the Word, Brian. Pray the Word."

Jesus did the same when he was tempted by Satan in the wilderness *Jesus, full of the Holy Spirit, left the Jordan and was led by the Spirit into the wilderness, where for forty days he was tempted by the devil. He ate nothing during those days, and at the end of them he was hungry. The devil said to him, "If you are the Son of God, tell this stone to become bread." Jesus answered, "It is written: 'Man shall not live on bread alone.'" The devil led him up to a high place and showed him in an instant all the kingdoms of the world. And he said to him, "I will give you all their authority and splendor; it has been given to me, and I can give it to anyone I want to. If you worship me, it will all be yours." Jesus answered, "It is written: 'Worship the Lord your God and serve him only.'" The devil led him to Jerusalem and had him stand on the highest point of the temple. "If you are the Son of God," he said, "throw yourself down from here. For it is written: "'He will command his angels concerning you to guard you carefully; they will lift you up in their hands, so that you will not strike your foot against a stone.'" Jesus answered, "It is said: 'Do not put the Lord your God to the test.* (Luke 4:1-12 NIV). He was the Son of God, but he did not use his divine authority. Instead, he used the authority of the Scriptures. Because this is such an important part of why this book even made sense for us to write is that we must mimic Christ in our life through application of the Word of God. Lean into the story and see how Jesus himself combatted the enemy when he was tempted. Read this over and over and use the Word to combat the enemy.

9. Memorize Scripture.

The most important key to a vibrant prayer life is to understand our spiritual authority in Christ as explained in the Scriptures. The only way to do that is to become intimately familiar with the Bible. Even a few minutes a day in the Word of God will add strength and authority to your prayers. Now, memorizing scripture can be done several different ways and you sort out which works best for you. It could be through song by adding a melody which works just like we teach children using songs. You can use acronyms to help you remember key words and phrases. Or you can even use cadence which is my method of choice in which I add movement to the words helps me remember it. There is no way that's perfect for everyone but choose one and use it regularly. You will create a reservoir of the word in the well of your heart that when needed you can draw from. You can only draw out the word that you have filled on the inside.

10 Prayers That Will Transform Your Finances

Does the state of your finances accelerate your pulse? Does your brain crunch number each night long after you're supposed to be asleep?

In our rapidly inflating and uncertain economy, money matters can drastically elevate our stress. Americans find themselves in debt, some to the tune of hundreds of thousands of dollars due to record layoffs, lost retirement accounts due to Ponzi schemes or even lessons learned from bad decisions.

It's hard to give generously or participate in short term missions when creditors are harassing us. We can't fully experience the abundant life Christ promised if we're buried in debt and enslaved to our fluctuating bank account.

If financial fears dominate your thoughts, be encouraged! Jesus isn't just the God of our salvation. He's our Jehovah-Jireh—our provider, guide, and ever-present help, and He longs to lead us into deeper levels of freedom in every area, including our finances. Here are 10 prayers that can help you align your heart, practices, and thus, finances, with God's perfect will.

1. Lord, help me trust You.

Obedience comes from surrender and surrender rests on trust. We may know, intellectually, that God is all-knowing, all-powerful, and has a good and loving plan for us. But we can lose sight of those truths when creditors come knocking or medical bills flood in. In those moments, our finite, easily distracted minds tend to focus on our problems rather than the God who loves us. The result—increased anxiety and decreased spiritual sensitivity.

The solution is redirecting our thoughts. Asking God to help and then choosing to trust He will. When chaos hits, we can feel as if we're victims to our circumstances—and our anxiety. But as we draw near to Christ in prayer, His Holy Spirit empowers, emboldens, and soothes, reminding us that He is our Jehovah-Jireh *And Abraham called the name of that place Jehovah Jireh: as it is said to this day, In the mount of the LORD it shall be seen.* (Genesis 22:14 KJV) and will meet all our needs according to His glorious riches in Christ Jesus *and my God will meet all your needs according to the riches of his glory in Christ Jesus. (Philippians 4:19 NIV).*

2. Lord, change my heart.

Sometimes financial struggles come from unexpected crises, but many times greed, selfishness, and impulsivity are to blame. We live in a consumer culture that celebrates instant gratification. As a result, we've grown accustomed to purchasing whatever we want whenever we want. Entitlement, and the undercurrent of discontentment that usually follows, can be difficult to fight. We work hard; why shouldn't we have that new car, larger home, or luxurious seven-day vacation?

There's nothing wrong with traveling or enjoying nice things—if our finances permit and our hearts are in tune with Christ. But if we're allowing our economic status to define or fulfill us, we've slipped into idolatry and therefore outside of God's will; that's a dangerous place to be, financially or otherwise. *When you ask, you do not receive, because you ask with wrong motives, that you may spend what you get on your pleasures.* (James 4:3 KJV)

If we want increased intimacy with God and the peace and clarity He offers, we need to ask Him to replace our idolatrous desires with a heart that beats only for Him.

3. Lord, grant me contentment.

I've found I need to repeat this prayer often—every time a covetous, discontent thought arises. When our kids were young, we lived in the Grandview, a suburb of KCMO, and I was surrounded by peers with much more money than we had (or at least, who routinely spent more than we did). Initially, we mirrored the practices of our friends and buried ourselves in debt. One Christmas, with maxed out credit cards and a nearly depleted bank account, we were forced to make a choice: apply for more credit or drastically change our habits.

Praise God, by His grace, we chose the latter, and our journey began with learning to be content. For us, this meant buying a used car instead of a newer one and driving it well past its glamorous stage. For Paul, the apostle who wrote the oft-quoted passage *I know what it is to be in need, and I know what it is to have plenty. I have learned the secret of being content in any and every situation, whether well fed or hungry, whether living in plenty or in want.* (Philippians 4:12 KJV) He learned the secret of being content when in plenty or in want, that meant cultivating joy while imprisoned and gratitude for whatever sliver of bread God provided.

That might seem harsh, perhaps even unrealistic, but it's interesting to note, Paul is also the man who wrote Philippians, the book on joy.

Could it be that contentment paves the way for joy, and in the process, financial freedom?

4. Lord, give me confidence.

I've often wondered what my spending would look like if I had no one to impress. If I lived on some remote island without other human contact, would I seriously care what I wore? What make of car I drove, or how well-decorated my little hut might appear? Though this line of thinking may seem silly, it illustrates an important premise—many of us spend money we don't have to impress others. Whether this involves buying a new car to appear more successful than we are or failing to say no when our friends suggest an expensive activity, this long-standing trend has landed many in debt.

The solution—become deeply grounded in who and whose—we are. Recognizing we're deeply loved, have a God-ordained purpose, and are valuable because of the price Christ was willing to pay for us helps insulate us from the people-pleasing trap—a path that inevitably leaves us emotionally, if not financially, bankrupt.

5. Lord, give me a generous heart.

Greed kills our relationships with others, our joy and peace, dulls our spiritual ears, and drastically hinders our intimacy with Christ. After all, how can we commune with the God who gave His everything so we could live if we're walking through that life with fisted hands? Moreover, why would He bless us materially when we're only going to use our wealth to gratify our desires?

Everything we have belongs to God to be used by Him for His glory. In light of this, consider Jesus' words in (Luke 16:11-12 NIV), *So if you have not been trustworthy in handling worldly wealth, who will trust you with true riches? And if you have not been trustworthy with someone else's property, who will give you property of your own?*

6. *God, help me live with integrity.*

We could easily repeat Jesus' words from (Luke 16:10 NIV) "Whoever *can be trusted with very little can also be trusted with much, and whoever is dishonest with very little will also be dishonest with much*. Everything we do or don't do both reveals and builds our character, and either reflects Christ or distorts His image.

Most of us probably would never seriously consider tax evasion or fraud but we might be tempted to behave deceptively in other, seemingly less consequential, situations. We may not think taking a handful of paper clips from the office or sending a personal fax or two is a big deal, but when God gave man the Ten Commandments, He didn't set up a sliding scale on honesty. To the contrary, Scripture says God hates all dishonesty and demands His followers live with the utmost integrity in all matters, including in how we manage our finances.

7. *Jesus, help me persevere.*

Creating a workable budget can be challenging. Living according to that budget for more than a few months can feel practically impossible, especially if we are attempting to climb out of debt. Spending habits take time to change, and though the tug not to impulse shop might grow easier, I suspect, in our consumer culture where we're bombarded with messages to buy-buy-buy, we'll always find it difficult to choose frugality over momentary pleasures.

Focusing on long-term goals, like buying or paying off a house or saving up for a vacation can help. As can praying for the strength to persevere, even if we find ourselves eating boxed macaroni and cheese more times than we care to count.

8. *God, help me align my priorities with Yours.*

When my spending and my income clash, it's almost always a sign that my priorities have become misaligned. Most likely I've begun to value material things above the spiritual. This is especially true when I can find the money to buy those cute shoes in the department store but never seem to have enough to pay my tithe.

Material pleasures aren't sinful, but if we value accessories more than helping to fund the expansion of God's kingdom, our appearance has a greater piece of our heart than Christ does. In (Matthew 6:24 NIV) Jesus told us what happens when we chase after material wealth while attempting to serve Christ. "Either you will hate the one and love the other, or you will be devoted to the one and despise the other," He said. "You cannot serve both God and money."

9. Jesus, help me develop a long-term focus.

That expensive steak dinner that tasted so great in the moment will likely be forgotten by tomorrow. That outfit we absolutely had to have today might land in our local thrift store by the year's end. And that new car we felt certain would give us such pleasure depreciated by $4,000 or more the moment we drove it off the lot. I don't have any statistics to share here, but it's been said that most of the things we spend money on ends up in sewage and landfills.

But every dollar we scrimp and save and put into savings will continue to work for us year after year. As will the money we invest in retirement or paying off our home. In life and finances the adage, "pay now or pay later," holds true. Scripture puts it this way, *A hard worker has plenty of food, but a person who chases fantasies ends up in poverty* (Proverbs 28:19 NLT) A hard worker has plenty of food, but a person who chases fantasies ends up in poverty. The trustworthy person will get a rich reward, but a person who wants quick riches will get into trouble). Granted, sometimes life hits hard, and financial difficulties hit despite our most diligent efforts, but focusing on where we want to be tomorrow, not simply what would make us happy today, makes economic stability more probable.

10. *God, center my thoughts and heart on the things of eternity.*

I've never been great at self-denial, and honestly, there are times when saving that dollar today so I can enjoy 10 tomorrow doesn't feel like reason enough—especially when my favorite coffee drink is on the line! Though my heart longs for things of enduring value, I'm easily pulled in by whatever screams the loudest or flashes the brightest. But then Jesus reminds me of my ultimate and most fulfilling purpose—to play a part in His redemptive mission—and suddenly all those items that once captivated me, suddenly fade as eternity shifts into focus.

Because when I'm standing in front of my Savior, and He asks me, "What did you do with the gifts I gave you," I'd like to be able to say more than simply, "I drank a lot of really great coffee."

5 Good Prayers for Rest from Busy-ness

If you feel too busy to rest. That's a telltale sign it's time to rest in God. Life was getting busy—too busy. Maybe you've been there: when you were always looking forward to the next event, no longer content in the moment. No sooner had I sent my next book manuscript to the publisher, when I began to ponder my next project. Everyone else seemed to ask me that as well, "What will you work on next?"

I habitually pushed forward, without taking enough time to relish and celebrate the victories along the way. And then COVID 19 happened, and everything shut down and you were like, "yes! This is it! I'm going to do nothing and it's going to be everything I thought it would be!" but then it turns out that nope, this is just my personality, not my circumstances.

During a women's retreat the following weekend, no less than a dozen women confirmed the direction

I sensed God was leading me: into a season of rest. REST? Why would I want to do that? I had things to write and talks to give. God knows my personality: I'd rather have three urgent projects going with barn-burning deadlines than be told to rest.

But God always knows best.

In the month after that retreat when I felt like He was leading me into a season of rest, I fulfilled my speaking commitments and visited my son at college. Upon returning home, my doctor called to tell me what no one likes nor wants to hear: "I needed surgery." Surgery was scheduled and treatment began. The physical toll was great, but God had prepared me for this time by clearing my calendar.

We become so consumed with accomplishing tasks, that we forget God can do more during times of rest than in our most "productive times." I used to think rest was a luxury. Now I realize it is crucial for warfare.

Pray the scriptures when you need the rest of God. It has great and many benefits:

1. In rest, God provides safety.
But now the Lord my God has given me rest on every side, and there is no adversary or disaster (1 Kings 5:4 ESV). The Lord sometimes needs us to rest in the security of our trust in Him.

2. Rest allows our bodies to heal. God desires healing for us.

Rest is a great thing to do for ourselves and others around us. He maketh me to lie down in green pastures: he leadeth me beside the still waters. He restoreth my soul: he leadeth me in the paths of righteousness for his name's sake. (Psalm 23:2-3 KJV)

3. Rest allows God the opportunity to teach us His ways, and as He teaches us, we learn to rest.

Come to me, all who labor and are heavy laden, and I will give you rest. Take my yoke upon you, and learn from me, for I am gentle and lowly in heart, and you will find rest for your souls. For my yoke is easy, and my burden is light. (Matthew 11:28-30 ESV)

4. We were created in God's image, and when we rest, we align ourselves with the very nature of God.

And on the seventh day God finished his work that he had done, and he rested on the seventh day from all his work that he had done. So, God blessed the seventh day and made it holy, because on it God rested from all his work that he had done in creation (Genesis 2:2-3 ESV).

5. Rest is a gift from God. We can rest in His presence.

And he said, "My presence will go with you, and I will give you rest. (Exodus 33:14 ESV).

You don't have to think of rest as lying-in bed only, but more so think also of the kind of peace and rest felt during times of prayer in His presence. Taking the time to rest requires trust in the One who commanded us to do so.

Jesus never hurried, and he modeled for us a lifestyle that included rest. If it was good enough for Jesus, shouldn't it be so for us also?

10 Prayers for Young Children

At some point, every parent reaches that place of realizing that we can't control everything, and we can't produce a lifetime of happy endings for our kids. But rather than throwing up our hands in defeat, a wise mom or dad gets on their knees and seeks the wisdom and help of God: the one who created your child and loves him even more than you do (it's true!). Here are some specific ways you can pray for your child and Scripture references to help you.

1. Pray for faith.

We do what we can to give our children a steady diet of the truth, but at some point, they must embrace a relationship with God on their own. *"Jesus grew in wisdom and stature and in favor with God and all the people."* (Luke 2:52 NIV) *"My sheep listen to my voice; I know them, and they follow me." "We want all of our children to know God intimately for themselves."* (John 10:27 NIV)

2. Pray for health.

It's something that moms and dads of healthy kids naturally take for granted, but that moms and dads of kids with serious health challenges value above all else except salvation. *"Praise the LORD, my soul, and forget not all his benefits—who forgives all your sins and heals all your diseases…"* (Psalm 103:2-3 NIV)

3. Pray for friendships.

Good friends are an important part of your child's social and emotional development and can play a major role in shaping their views. *"The righteous choose their friends carefully, but the way of the wicked leads them astray."* (Proverbs 12:26 NIV) Now, I'm going to add on here a little bit because we now have young adult children and how they responded to those friends we liked and the friends we didn't. You'll need to present biblical truth instead of just saying, "I don't like those people." Because that can and will incite rebellion which you really do not want.

4. Pray for a future.

Your little one may still be a part of the crayons-and-paste set now, but the years go by quickly and they're suddenly out there making a life for themselves. Pray now for their preparation for what lies ahead and God's blessing. *Being confident of this, that he who began a good work in you will carry it on to completion until the day of Christ Jesus.* (Philippians 1:6 KJV)

5. Pray for character.

A child with a strong sense of right and wrong will make better choices and be spared many of the potential sorrows of poorer ones. Pray that they will embrace a life of integrity and goodness, even in childhood. *Therefore, my dear brothers, stand firm. Let nothing move you. Always give yourselves fully to the work of the Lord because you know that your labor in the Lord is not in vain.* (1 Corinthians 15:58 KJV). With that, it's important to teach your children about right in wrong in God's way that they will be able to be more than just good people, but rather God's people. *Train up a child in the way he should go and when he is old, he will not depart from it.* (Proverbs 22:6 NIV) We want our children to have a good understanding of who God and how living his way produces good character.

6. Pray for safety.

Even as they suffer playground bullies and struggle to ride a two-wheeler, asking for God's hand of protection—physical, emotional, and spiritual—over your child is always a good idea. *"I will lie down and sleep in peace, for you alone, O LORD, make me dwell in safety."* (Psalm 4:8 NIV) *The name of the LORD is a strong tower; the righteous run to it and are safe.* (Proverbs 18:10 KJV)

7. Pray for joy and peace.

No amount of money or success will ever bring your child happiness unless they learn to be content in a variety of circumstances. Real joy is a fruit of the Holy Spirit along with peace. It can change our perspectives, even in our situations. *"But the fruit of the Spirit is love, joy, peace, longsuffering, gentleness, goodness, faith, Meekness, temperance: against such there is no law."* (Galatians 5:22-23 KJV) *"I am not saying this because I am in need, for I have learned to be content whatever the circumstances."* (Philippians 4:11 KJV) *"But godliness with contentment is great gain."* (1 Timothy 6:6 KJV)

8. Pray for their desire for the things that matter.

It's hard to articulate to younger children because the things of the world are fleeting, and that eternal things are those you can build a meaningful life around. Pray for God to show you how to live this idea daily in front of them and for them to be able to understand it. *"So, we fix our eyes not on what is seen, but on what is unseen, since what is seen is temporary, but what is unseen is eternal."* (2 Corinthians 4:18 KJV)

9. Pray for purity.

For children, the battle for purity is largely a battle for their minds: keeping the multitude of negative influences and ideas that are shouted at them daily by the media at bay. Pray for God's guidance and help in keeping your kids pure in thought and deed. *"Finally, brothers and sisters, whatever is true, whatever is noble, whatever is right, whatever is pure, whatever is lovely, whatever is admirable—if anything is excellent or praiseworthy—think about such things."* (Philippians 4:8 KJV) Lastly, and we never want to negate the importance of the relationships our children have with others in our family and their friends. Be cautious and ask the Lord for a discerning spirit. *"Do not be deceived: Evil company corrupts good habits."* (1 Corinthians 15:33 KJV)

10. Pray for their future spouses.

It may sound crazy to pray about something that's twenty years in the future, but out there, somewhere, is another child who may one day bring all their baggage, good and bad, into your child's life. Pray for God to provide the right mate for your child, and that they would enjoy a healthy marriage rooted in a strong common faith. I want to go just a little deeper here. As a parent, you know your child's strengths and you know their weaknesses. God has the perfect person already to greatly compliment your child in their walk with Him.

Pray that the road to their meeting will be beautiful and not painful. Many times, young adults may become distracted and lose focus.

Pray for both of their hearts to be prepared to serve each other in Holy Union and have a desire to please and submit to the other. A marriage can greatly increase a ministry, but it can also greatly hinder a ministry.

Teach your child now what they should look for in a spouse. The Bible says a virtuous woman's price is far above rubies. Your daughter should know her virtue and your son should recognize a virtuous woman over all others.

The Bible also says that a man that fears the Lord shall be mighty upon the earth. Your son should understand what it means to have a healthy fear and respect for the Lord. He should understand what it means to submit and be humble. Likewise, your daughter should as well. A man who respects and fears the Lord will lead his family in the right direction in life. *"Praise ye the Lord. Blessed is the man that feareth the Lord that delighteth greatly in his commandments. His seed shall be mighty upon earth: the generation of the upright shall be blessed."* (Psalms 112:1-2 **KJV**)

This has become increasingly more of my prayer as our children have gotten to be young adults and dating. I still pray this pray unto the Lord earnestly. Marriage is for a lifetime and my prayer is that it'll be lasting, loving and Christ like for them and for us as in-laws.

15+ Prayers for Teens & Young Adult Children

O n a very personal note, at some point I took my "Super Mom" cape off and embraced the fact that life had suddenly become a lot bigger than Band-Aids and notes in their lunchbox—a lot bigger than what I could easily fix. Our three children, now in their late adolescence and early adulthood years, old need us in a greater capacity than we've known before. Our relationship with each of them is different for them and different for us.

The teen and young adult years aren't just hard on kids. They're hard on moms and dads too. The years can leave us feeling as left out and as inadequate as they do our kids. And because now we can't always provide a quick remedy, we can feel like we're failing as a parent. This has caused me to change how I pray for my children and the children of others. I've never prayed more for my kids, and for myself, as I have during their teen and young adult years. Considering broken friendships, tainted television, and social media, I MUST pray. Prayers that in the past I would keep to myself, I now share with close friends and ask them to pray with me. (Boy does it help to know others are going through the same thing.) My prayers have become more desperate—a heart crying out because it needs God to do what only He can do.

So, here are prayers as they have become a continuous conversation. I now completely understand the guidance of "pray without ceasing". It has taken up significant residence in my heart. I pray as I'm falling asleep. I pray in my car. Sometimes, I drive by their schools or workplaces, just to pray. I pray on my front porch as they're leaving with their friends. (Watching my son drive off to college or my daughter and her new driver's license, triggers intense prayer time!) The more they've grown, I find the more my prayer life has grown as well.

I now say…

I pray, Lord, for healthy friendships with others who are on the same Godly path with them.

I pray, Lord, that you would help them to be watchful of others, discerning their spirits to know who their friends really are and who may disappoint them.

I pray, Lord, for the person each of them will marry. I pray that you will send them mates that You have prepared for them.

I pray, Lord, for guidance as they pursue college and jobs.

I pray, Lord, for protection over their minds and hearts as they live in the world, but not of the world.

I pray, Lord, for courage to be who You made them to be.

I pray, Lord, for wisdom in all their choices.

I pray, Lord, that they will trust in a bigger plan when things aren't going "right."

I pray, Lord, for joy amid confusion and hurt.

I pray, Lord, that You will be their source and the Bible will be their standard for living.

I pray, Lord, that they will choose You for themselves all the days of their lives.

I pray, Lord, that their testimony will be that they have loved You all the days of their lives and that they learn from the mistakes of others rather than a prodigal experience.

I pray, Lord, that their hearts will be filled with love to fulfill Your command to love You and others as they do themselves.

I pray, Lord, that they will hear from You and obey You promptly.

I pray, Lord, that they are protected in their travels to and from everywhere they go.

I pray, Lord, that they would go to an institution of learning for their trade or profession at low or no cost.

Prayer for Older, Adult Sons and Daughters

Y ou too may want to continue to encourage your adult sons and daughters while they have the freedom to make their own choices. But where do you draw the line between helping them to build their own lives well and enabling them to remain dependent on you? And how do you deal with all your many concerns about them—from their friendships and romantic partnerships, to their career pursuits and financial management? The goal here is that you raise your children to be adults who can take good care of themselves and their families. It is not for parents to rule over their adult sons or daughter's life, but rather to guide them towards the Lord and seek the Lord on their behalf.

Prayer is the key. Praying for your adult sons and daughters will connect you to the only perfect Parent, God. Pray that they will invite Him to act powerfully in their lives. I am believing that God will give us everything we need as our children become adults, but more importantly that they seek God for themselves and you're there to support and encourage.

Pray that your adult sons and daughters will...

1. See God pour out His Spirit on them:
Ask God to give your adult sons and daughters the faith to seek Him and welcome an outpouring of the Holy Spirit into their lives. Pray that they will understand the Holy Spirit's power, and that they will follow the Spirit's guidance so they can recognize the difference between what's true and what's false. Ask God to empower them through His Spirit so they'll be able to live faithfully.

2. Develop a heart for God, His Word, and His Ways:
Ask God to turn your adult sons' and daughters' hearts toward Him and open them to receive His love. Pray for their desire to know God better and become more like Him. Ask God to bring them to repentance about their sins. Pray that God will close their hearts to evil lies and open them to His truth. Ask God to give them a passion to read, study, reflect on, and memorize Scripture. Tell them stories of how God has worked in your life (such as how He has answered some key prayers), also describe what your relationship with Him means to you. Point out the good qualities you see in them as people and help them discover and fulfill God's good purposes for their lives.

3. Grow in wisdom, discernment, and revelation:
Wisdom will empower your adult sons and daughters to see the consequences of their actions before they act, enabling them to make the right decisions about actions to take. Pray that they will have the wisdom to fear God, speak the right words to others, avoid blaspheming God's name, be humble rather than prideful, avoid being drawn into the world's concept of wisdom, love the Bible, and always seek the counsel of godly and wise people.

Discernment will enable your adult sons and daughters to understand what would normally be obscure to them. It will help them see what's good and what's evil, see what's holy and what's sinful, see what's right and what's wrong, choose to do what's right in any situation, and understand more about God's ways.

Revelation is knowledge God can give to your adult sons and daughters that they wouldn't have had otherwise. It gives them a vision for their lives, understanding and enlightenment about their purpose and calling, empowers them to respond to their circumstances in the right ways that will protect them from disastrous decisions, and helps them see who God is more clearly. Pray for God to give your adult sons and daughters the benefit of these qualities every day of their lives.

4. Find freedom, restoration, and wholeness: Whenever your adult sons and daughters are struggling with a specific, sinful attitude or action, your prayers can be instrumental in helping them find the healing they need. Ask God to set them free from anything that separates them from Him. Pray for them to find the transformation that can only be found in God's presence. Ask God to help them establish the disciplines of reading the Bible, praying, and praising and worshiping Him regularly, since God uses those experiences to changes people's lives for the better. Pray for the healing you need in your own life so your adult sons and daughters can see through your life a powerful example of how God is at work. Ask God to take anything in your adult children's lives that is currently broken and make it whole.

5. Understand God's purpose for their lives: Ask God to help your adult sons and daughters figure out the best direction they should go with their lives. Pray for the Holy Spirit to guide them as they make decisions, from where to go to college to what career and volunteer work to pursue. Ask God to help them discover, develop, and use the gifts and talents He has given them. Pray for God to encourage them and clear away confusion when they become overwhelmed or fail, so they can hear from His Spirit in fresh ways and keep fulfilling His purposes for their lives. Ask God to instill a desire in them to always be in the center of His will.

*6. **Work successfully and have financial stability:*** Ask God to give your adult sons and daughters a strong desire to be diligent and work hard, always giving their best effort to the tasks they undertake. Pray that they will be able to earn an income that meets their needs. Also pray that they will: always work when opportunities arise; have the wisdom they need to save money for tough times; learn to give generously to support God's work on earth; seek God about everything, including the financial provision they need; gain wealth according to God's will; know that true treasure is found in God; and always have a sense of what is right and ethical about managing money.

*7. **Have a sound mind and a right attitude:*** Ask God to help your adult sons and daughters make the right choices about what they allow into their minds, so they'll have nothing less than the sound minds He has given them. Pray that God will protect them from having evil fill their minds with lies that oppress them mentally and emotionally. Ask God to dissolve bad attitudes in their minds, such as pride, fear, anger, anxiety, and a broken heart. Encourage your adult sons and daughters to develop a habit of praising God regularly, since that practice will heal their minds, emotions, and attitudes. Pray for Christ's peace to flood their souls and rule in their hearts every day.

8. Resist evil influences and destructive behavior:
Ask God to give each of your adult sons and daughters
a humble, repentant, and teachable spirit. Pray for
God to destroy any spirit of rebellion in their lives.
God's love and grace will always be available to your
children, no matter what they've done. Ask God to
help them return to Him after they've strayed. Pray
that God will open their eyes to see the truth and
not be blinded by evil lies, they can hear God's voice
leading them, their hearts will be filled with wisdom
and knowledge, they will turn away from evil when
they encounter it, they will understand that they
are engaged in a spiritual battle every day, they will
respond to trials by turning to God, and they will
learn to praise God for the healing and deliverance
He has for them.

9. Avoid all sexual pollution and temptation: Ask
God to give your adult sons and daughters a fresh
outpouring of the Holy Spirit on them to cause them
to see the world from God's perspective and can
better resist an attack of lust. Pray that they will have
a renewed heart for God, His Word, and His ways;
have wisdom, discernment, and revelation about how
to avoid sexual pollution; find freedom, restoration,
and wholeness from whatever has already sexually
polluted them; refuse to look at whatever is offensive
to God and harmful to them; focus on the path and
purpose God has for them; recognize the power of

lust to destroy their souls; understand that lust in any form is against God's will; live in the Spirit of God and not in the lust of the flesh; and run to God and the truth of His Word whenever they're tempted to be drawn into sexual pollution of any kind.

10. Experience good health and God's healing: If your adult sons and daughters are in good health now, ask God to show them what to do to maintain good health: what to eat, how to exercise, and how to get rejuvenating sleep. Pray that they will have the discernment to know what's good and what's bad for them, the wisdom to make right choices, and the revelation about what is right for their bodies. If they're struggling with bad health brought on by sickness or injury, point them to Jesus as their healer and never stop praying for their complete healing, regardless of the severity of their medical prognosis. Ask God to give you and your adult sons and daughters the faith you need to pray boldly for healing and help you not lose heart or hope. Encourage your adult sons and daughters to trust God to answer your prayers according to what's best.

11. Pray for a Godly marriage if they choose to marry: Pray that your adult sons and daughters will marry fellow believers who are sexually pure before marriage and have godly character. Pray that they will have strong relationships with their in-laws.

Minister Brian & Michelle Gines   137

12. Pray that they'll raise godly children if they choose to have children: Ask God to help your adult sons and daughters be good parents by recognizing that their children are gifts from God, training their children in God's ways, teaching their children with love rather than anger, disciplining their children wisely and diligently, and obey God's ways while raising their children so their prayers will be answered. Pray that you'll be understanding and respectful of their wishes if they choose not to have children.

13. Maintain strong and fulfilling relationships: Ask God to help your adult sons and daughters develop good relationships with godly friends; coworkers; and family members like their siblings and cousins, you and your spouse, and extended family. Pray that God will remove people from their lives who are bad influences on them. Ask God to help your adult sons and daughters pursue forgiveness and reconciliation to fix broken relationships with others.

14. Be protected and survive tough times: Pray that your adult sons and daughters will have long and fruitful lives. Ask God to protect them from falling victim to manifestations of evil. Pray that they will have the wisdom and judgment to do what's right in every situation, learn to fear God and not other people, trust God and His Word, live in the presence of God where there is safety, make God their refuge and turn to Him for protection, use God's Word as their shield from evil attacks, refuse to live in fear of danger or disease – even when they see destruction and death happening around them, understand the consequences for not living God's way, and understand that the reward for living God's way is protection.

15. *Ask God to surround your adult sons and daughters with ministering angels.* Whenever your adult sons and daughters are going through a tough time, pray that they will be aware of God's presence with them and rely on His strength to get through it well. Ask God to bring something good for them out of even the worst situations.

16. *Walk into the future that God has for them:* Ask God to help your adult sons and daughters rely on His guidance every day so they can discover the peaceful and hopeful lives He wants them to live. Pray for God to give them the strength and opportunities they need to fulfill His purposes for their lives. Ask God to help them remain faithful and keep growing through their whole lifetimes. Remember that, in Christ, nothing can ever separate them from God's love.

Prayers for Our Parents as They Age

Honoring parents means more than sending cards on special days. And it's more than an occasional invitation to dinner. It is interceding for those who have interceded for us. One of the greatest things we can do for our parents is to offer them up to the Lord in prayer.

In the biblical context, *Honor your father and your mother, so that you may live long in the land the Lord your God is giving you.* (Exodus 20:12 NIV) a*nd Honor your father and mother—which is the first commandment with a promise* (Ephesians 6:2 NIV), it includes respect and a commitment of grown children to care for their parents, especially when they are infirmed. It is one beautiful outworking of the Gospel. God cares for us, His children, and He models what ongoing, compassionate ministry looks like.

One of the greatest privileges of my adult life has been to pray for my mother and Jerry along with Brian's parents. My mother and father-in-law recently moved back to our area after 20 years due to health concerns and to be closer to family. We now have the privilege of seeing and serving each of them more often. When we got married and up until a year ago, we all never lived in the same city. But now, they're only a 5-minute drive away from us. But one thing we could do no matter what distance they are from us, is pray. I've been able to watch and learn from my mother-in-law over the years. She is an intercessor and prayer warrior for the masses. She has a ministry in her heart and a divine calling to prayer. I've gleaned from her passion and have been witness to beautiful and peaceful results of a life of prayer, especially for the family. My own mother has been equally instrumental in pushing me to pray. She birthed me when she was just a teenage girl. Without having to say another word, you can all understand that prayer has been important in our lives. Even when we didn't have a real knowledge or vocabulary around praying. We had it within our hearts and spirit until such time as it has evolved for both of us.

As we begin to see our parents' age it becomes even more important that we cover them in prayer. Here are some of the things I've found useful to pray over the years. Perhaps it will be a blessing to you for your parent(s).

1. *Lord I pray for your continuing PROVIDENCE in my parent's life.*

I am grateful my parent(s) trusted in You long ago. Let their latter be even greater than their past. As well, I pray for the parents and elderly loved ones who still do not know you, Lord, and I ask you to bring them to Yourself and bring about their salvation and transformation in their lives. *For it is by grace you have been saved, through faith—and this is not from yourselves, it is the gift of God— 9 not by works, so that no one can boast.* (Ephesians 2:8-9 NIV)*; He has saved us and called us to a holy life—not because of anything we have done but because of his own purpose and grace. This grace was given us in Christ Jesus before the beginning of time,* (2 Timothy 1:9 KJV)

Lord I pray, You will bring to my loved one's remembrance all the ways You have been their hope and help—in many cases since childhood. *My soul, wait thou only upon God; for my expectation is from him.* (Psalm 62:5) *For thou art my hope, O Lord GOD: thou art my trust from my youth.* (Psalm 71:5 KJV)

I thank you for all the ways You used my parent(s) to shape my young life. What a precious gift! My parent(s) guided me in practical ways and showed me how to trust You. Although my parent was not perfect, I sensed the desire to mold me into a good person, and I'm thankful I was encouraged to become a Christ-follower.

Or for parents that did not offer encouragement in the things of God. I pray for them Lord. I pray and thank you for keeping me when it was difficult. I pray now for my parent(s) who did not honor you in my upbringing that you still have given me opportunity to learn of you and I pray for them anyway. They may not have shown me the way, but I thank you for being my Father (my parent).

And now the roles are reversed. I have the privilege to help and serve, and remind my loved one of Your tender, shepherding care. Give me patience, wisdom, and an understanding heart. Help me continue to show respect and appreciation, and to value who You, in Your Providence, created my loved one to be *Honour thy father and thy mother: that thy days may be long upon the land which the LORD thy God giveth thee.* (Exodus 20:12 KJV). Ultimately, I know Your care for my parent is beyond anything I can offer, for every good gift comes from You *Blessed is the man that endureth temptation: for when he is tried, he shall receive the crown of life, which the Lord hath promised to them that love him.* (James 1:17 KJV).

2. I pray for PROTECTION for my parent(s).

I pray my parent will keep on leaning on You, the Rock of strength and righteousness *Be thou my strong habitation, whereunto I may continually resort:* (Psalm 71:3a KJV). *My flesh and my heart faileth: but God is the strength of my heart, and my portion for ever (Psalm*.73:26 KJV). Spread your protection over my parent because You are the ultimate Refuge. *But let all those that put their trust in thee rejoice let them ever shout for joy, because thou defendest them: let them also that love thy name be joyful in thee.* (Psalm 5:11 KJV).

I ask you to protect my parent from the evil one and show the way out in moments of temptation, *"But the Lord is faithful, who shall stablish you, and keep you from evil.* (2 Thessalonians 3:3 KJV). *There hath no temptation taken you but such as is common to man: but God is faithful, who will not suffer you to be tempted above that ye are able; but will with the temptation also make a way to escape, that ye may be able to bear it.* (1 Corinthians 10:13 KJV). May wisdom, discretion and understanding protect and guide every day *Forsake her not, and she shall preserve thee: love her, and she shall keep thee.* (Proverbs 4:6 KJV). *Discretion shall preserve thee, understanding shall keep thee:* Proverbs 2:11 KJV).

I pray my parent will be courageous, confident in Your presence, help and deliverance. *"I will lift up my eyes to the mountains; From where shall my help come? My help comes from the LORD, Who made heaven and earth. He will not allow your foot to slip; He who keeps you will not slumber. Behold, He who keeps Israel Will neither slumber nor sleep. The LORD is your keeper; The LORD is your shade on your right hand. The sun will*

*not smite you by day, Nor the moon by night. The LORD
will protect you from all evil; He will keep your soul.
The LORD will guard your going out and your coming
in From this time forth and forever."* (Psalm 121:1-8
KJV). *"Be strong and of a good courage, fear not, nor
be afraid of them: for the LORD thy God, he it is that
doth go with thee; he will not fail thee, nor forsake thee."*
(Deuteronomy 31:6 KJV).

3. I pray for PROVISION—that you will meet my parent's needs.

Show me how to meet my parent's needs in ways that
will please You, Lord. Equip me to be a good steward
in my loved one's care. *"For it is sanctified by the word
of God and prayer."* (1 Timothy 4:5 KJV) "Do *not
sharply rebuke an older man, but rather appeal to him as a
father, to the younger men as brothers, 2the older women as
mothers, and the younger women as sisters, in all purity."*
(1 Timothy 5:1-2 KJV).

There is much I can do, but You are the Great
Provider. Thank you for your willingness and
faithfulness to supply my parent's needs for Your
glory and my loved one's joy. *"He that spared not his
own Son, but delivered him up for us all, how shall he
not with him also freely give us all things?"* (Romans
8:32 KJV). *"Do not worry then, saying, 'What will we
eat?' or 'What will we drink?' or 'What will we wear
for clothing?'" "For the Gentiles eagerly seek all these*

things; for your heavenly Father knows that you need all these things." (Matthew 6:31-32 KJV). *"But my God shall supply all your need according to his riches in glory by Christ Jesus."* (Philippians 4:19 KJV). I pray my parent will be made holy through Your grace and receive Your good favor. *"Now may the God of peace Himself sanctify you entirely; and may your spirit and soul and body be preserved complete, without blame at the coming of our Lord Jesus Christ. Faithful is He who calls you, and He also will bring it to pass."* (1 Thessalonians 5:23-24 KJV) *"For the LORD God is a sun and shield: the LORD will give grace and glory: no good thing will he withhold from them that walk uprightly."* (Psalm 84:11 KJV).

4. I pray for POWER, your strength in my parent's weakness.

As strength declines, I pray for a greater sense of Your presence and power. *"Cast me not off in the time of old age; forsake me not when my strength faileth."* (Psalm 71:9 KJV). You are mighty, Father, and our strength is in You alone. *"Finally, my brethren, be strong in the Lord, and in the power of his might."* (Ephesians 6:10 KJV). In times of need, help my parent lean on your sufficiency and everlasting arms. *"And God is able to make all grace abound toward you; that ye, always having all sufficiency in all things, may abound to every good work:"* (2 Corinthians 9:8 KJV) *"The eternal God is thy refuge, and underneath are the everlasting arms: and he shall thrust out the enemy from before thee;*

and shall say, Destroy them." (Deuteronomy 33:27 KJV); and when life feels so impossible, remind my loved one that nothing is impossible with You. *"But Jesus beheld them, and said unto them, With men this is impossible; but with God all things are possible."* (Matthew 19:26 KJV).

5. *I pray for PEACE in my parent's aging years.*

I ask You to give my parent a trusting and thankful heart, especially as days grow more difficult. *In everything give thanks: for this is the will of God in Christ Jesus concerning you.* (1 Thessalonians 5:18 KJV). Help my aging parent take every disappointment to You. Preserve them from any bitterness or spirit of discontent. *Let integrity and uprightness preserve me; for I wait on thee.* (Psalm 25:21 KJV).

6. *I pray for grace in their aging process.*

I pray the Holy Spirit will bring comfort, guidance, and calm. *"Howbeit when he, the Spirit of truth, is come, he will guide you into all truth: for he shall not speak of himself; but whatsoever he shall hear, that shall he speak, and he will shew you things to come."* (John 16:13 KJV) *"Who comforteth us in all our tribulation, that we may be able to comfort them which are in any trouble, by the comfort wherewith we ourselves are comforted of God."* (2 Corinthians 1:4 KJV), and that my parent will not become discouraged in aging.

7. *I pray for continuing PURPOSE.*

I ask you to help my parent(s) flourish— "like the palm tree... bearing fruit in their old age"—with an eternal perspective. *"The righteous man will flourish like the palm tree; He will grow like a cedar in Lebanon. Planted in the house of the LORD, They will flourish in the courts of our God. They will still yield fruit in old age; They shall be full of sap and very green, To declare that the LORD is upright;*

He is my rock, and there is no unrighteousness in Him." (Psalm 92:12-15 KJV). Work in my loved one's life for Your glory. *"For which cause we faint not; but though our outward man perish, yet the inward man is renewed day by day."* (2 Corinthians 4:16 KJV). Open appropriate opportunities for ministry and influence.

Help my parent(s) live as a holy and faithful role model, Father, for as long as you allow. *"Older men are to be temperate, dignified, sensible, sound in faith, in love, in perseverance. Older women likewise are to be reverent in their behavior, not malicious gossips nor enslaved to much wine, teaching what is good, 4so that they may encourage the young women to love their husbands, to love their children,"* (Titus 2:2 KJV).

8. *I pray for their legacy to remain.*

I pray my parent(s), from a wealth of experience, will impart important life lessons You still want me to learn.

Fill my parent(s) mouth with Your praise, and a desire to worship and bring You glory from a testimony strong and true. *"Let my mouth be filled with thy praise and with thy honour all the day."* (Psalm 71:8 **KJV**).

Thank you for the many ways my parent(s) can influence children and grandchildren for good. I pray my loved one will, by word and deed, proclaim Your power and care to the next generation. *"Now also when I am old and greyheaded, O God, forsake me not; until I have shewed thy strength unto this generation, and thy power to every one that is to come."* (Psalm 71:18 **KJV**).

Father, I thank you for Jesus, who makes possible our God-honoring transition from this world to everlasting glory. As I pray these things for my parent, I pray them for myself as well. I pray we all will someday hear Your "well done." Amen!

Our Secret Weapon of Prayer
(Prayer is our Dragon Slayer)

I love in scripture in when Jesus went away to pray because it shows that just like you and me, He too, needed time away for prayer. *"But Jesus Himself would often slip away to the wilderness and pray."* (Luke 5:16 AMP). Jesus needed a break from the demands of his busy life to recharge His batteries and spend time with His Heavenly Father. The life of Christ is intended to give us examples we can follow and learn from. So, even though He was God incarnate, Jesus didn't draw on His superpowers as the Son of God when it came to facing life's challenges. Instead, when He was exhausted or burdened or in need of spiritual refreshment, He would "slip away" to pray — plugging into the power, perception, and purpose that can only be found in God's presence.

I call this intentional withdrawal. There are many that believe they can do it all without God's help, but I know firsthand that ALL my help comes from God above. When I can't... He can! Now, I want to emphasize with this principle because it can be misrepresented. It's often applied as, "I'm going to do everything I can possibly think of and then when that doesn't work, I'll finally ask God as a last resort," and that's not really a good practice for us. God wants us to turn to Him first.

Prayer is one of the most powerful weapons God has given us, and looking ahead, I believe it has never been more important for God's people to be on our knees. But knowing how to pray is not always easy. Jesus' disciples felt the same confusion. They were familiar with the oft-repeated prayers of the Torah, but Jesus prayed with a kind of authority and power they had never seen before—as though God was listening! So, when they came to Jesus, as told in Matthew 6, they didn't say, 'Teach us another prayer.' They said, *"Lord, teach us to pray."*

The Lord's Prayer (Matthew 6:9-13) is Christ's response. It is a beautiful prayer and one that every Christian should hide in their heart. But elegant as the words are, I do not believe Jesus intended it to become another ritualistic prayer. Rather, it was to be an example of how to pray.

The Lord's Prayer (Matthew 6:9-13 KJV)

Our Father which art in heaven, Hallowed be thy name. Thy kingdom come, Thy will be done in earth, as it is in heaven. Give us this day our daily bread. And forgive us our debts, as we forgive our debtors. And lead us not into temptation but deliver us from evil: For thine is the kingdom, and the power, and the glory, forever. Amen.

The Lord's Prayer: Luke 11:2-4 (KJV)

Our Father which art in heaven, Hallowed be thy name. Thy kingdom come. Thy will be done, as in heaven, so in earth. Give us day by day our daily bread. And forgive us our sins; for we also forgive every one that is indebted to us. And lead us not into temptation; but deliver us from evil.

The Lord showed us how to pray, war and fight in the spirit. He has left us His Word to equip us with what we need along with power, love and a strong mind; no fear. We can go to the Lord in prayer with full confidence that He is on our side. When we pray God hears us and Jesus is interceding on our behalf.

Keep Tending your Fire of Prayer

The fire shall ever be burning upon the altar;
it shall never go out. (Lev. 6:13 KJV)

Pray without ceasing (1 Thess. 5:17 KJV)

The scriptures are clear, wouldn't you agree? Do not stop praying and don't let the fire go out of it. It is a vital element; for your marriage, life, family, and everything that pertains to you.

God gave this instruction to the Old Testament priests. If that wasn't enough, He also called His people to offer ceaseless sacrifices—burning bloody, slain animals, day after day, morning, and evening.

God gives us helpful pictures in His Word so that we may better understand the nature and purposes of His commands. Here, the fire represents the presence of God, always emanating, or "burning" with, holiness and purity. The animal sacrifices depict the necessary payment for sin. God's people placed these atoning sacrifices on the altar and watched the flames consume them. How was this perpetually possible? The priests obeyed God's command to tend the fire, and God graciously dwelt with His (unholy and undeserving) people.

Today, we no longer need to sacrifice animals before coming into God's presence. Since Christ gave himself as a once-for-all sacrifice. *"For then must he often have suffered since the foundation of the world: but now once in the end of the world hath he appeared to put away sin by the sacrifice of himself. And as it is appointed unto men once to die, but after this the judgment: So, Christ was once offered to bear the sins of many; and unto them that look for him shall he appear the second time without sin unto salvation."* (Hebrews 9:26-28 KJV), those who put their faith in him can freely enter God's presence, day after day, morning, and evening. The Old Testament sacrificial system pointed to Christ but is no longer necessary considering Christ's completed, atoning work on the cross.

Spiritual Fire

While there is no longer a physical fire that we must tend to, there is most certainly a spiritual one for today's "royal priesthood"—Peter's remarkable name for Christian believers. *"But ye are a chosen generation, a royal priesthood, an holy nation, a peculiar people; that ye should shew forth the praises of him who hath called you out of darkness into his marvelous light;"* (1 Peter 2:9 KJV). The Levitical priests' task reminds us of Paul's exhortation to another perpetual action: to *pray without ceasing* (1 Thessalonians 5:17 KJV). Similarly, C.H. Spurgeon applies (Leviticus 6:13) to Christians, challenging them "keep the altar of private prayer burning." [6]

While the Bible tells us that we are "priests", we serve a great high priest, who is God. Hear Christ's compassionate invitation: *"For we do not have a high priest who is unable to sympathize with our weaknesses, but one who in every respect has been tempted as we are, yet without sin. Let us then with confidence draw near to the throne of grace, that we may receive mercy and find grace to help in time of need."* (Hebrews 4:15-16 KJV)

In the scripture, God initiates the physical fire. *"And there came a fire out from before the Lord, and consumed upon the altar the burnt offering and the fat: which when all the people saw, they shouted, and fell on their faces."* (Leviticus 9:24 KJV). He is the fire-starter. Likewise, he is the initiator of our devotion to him today. The Holy Spirit moves in our hearts to grant us the faith to trust in Christ. *We love the Lord because he first loved us* (1 Jn. 4:19 NIV). Knowing that the great high priest changes our hearts, we look to him to ignite in us a fresh love for him and a greater desire to commune with him.

There is common ground between the Old Testament priests tending a physical fire and today's "royal

---

[6] C.H. Spurgeon, Morning & Evening (Hendrickson Publishers, 1995), 394.

priesthood" of believers who mind a spiritual fire on the altar of private prayer. Both require hard work. Prayer takes effort. Praying "without ceasing" is a tall order—a solitary battle won or lost each day. It is a battle worth fighting.

Unpretentious Devotion

To pray without ceasing is not the call to never stop talking, but rather it is carrying a sense of prayerfulness into every aspect of our lives. I have heard it described as an open phone line with the Lord, where we never have to hang up. It is an awareness of being in his presence throughout each day. From the time we wake up until our heads hit the pillow, the Lord wants us to be conscious of His presence.

Regular, frequent, and undisturbed prayer is one of the most difficult things we are called to in the Christian life. Yet we know by experience that nothing worth doing comes easily. Spurgeon rightly says that "[secret] devotion is the very essence, evidence, and barometer, of vital...religion." [7]All other aspects of our lives borrow from the vibrancy of our time spent in personal fellowship with the Lord.

Devotion to private prayer comes with the cost of our time, our focus, and our pride. We do not like to be dependent, but isn't that how the Christian life works?

[7] C.H. Spurgeon, ibid

While we often function as if we are self-sufficient, the truth is that we are human, and therefore wholly dependent. Prayer is the best reminder of our right relation to God. Not even Jesus Christ operated apart from dependence on the Holy Spirit and prayer. The Holy Spirit was Jesus' inseparable companion, and the same Spirit who empowered our Lord, Jesus Christ is the Spirit who lives within all believers and enables us to commune with God.

Private prayer is the most beautiful posture and priority in the life of a believer because it tells the truth about our position before God. It reflects the fact that we are not the authors of our lives; rather, we depend on God for our every breath. Private prayer instructs our hearts to this end. It also operationalizes the mysterious reality that the God who holds all things together. *And he is before all things, and by him all things consist.* (Colossians 1:17 KJV) also wants to spend intimate one-on-one time with us. He wants to intentionally commune with us every day, throughout the day. We can have no greater audience than a private exchange with the living God.

A Priority and a Privilege

In addition to tending the fire, God instructed the Old Testament priests to regularly remove the ashes of each burnt offering. This task was a priority in order that the fire would stay ablaze. What ashes are accumulating on the fire of our secret devotion to God? God does not want our lukewarm hearts, so we must examine what smothers the flames. It may be the concerns of daily life, a long to-do list, unforgiveness, or unrepentant sin. It is time to lay those things aside.

One of the best ways to reignite a fire that once burned brightly is to open the Bible. Spending time with God's people and listening to sermons are good things, but they are no substitute for independently digging into God's Word. As Scripture reminds us of who God is, what he has done for us, and why he deserves our wholehearted devotion, we will be more motivated to spend daily time in his presence.

Prioritizing private prayer will help us to live for God's glory and receive the greatest joy and satisfaction from our communion with him. When we spend time in God's presence, and are reminded of biblical truths, the burden of prayer transforms into the privilege of prayer.

But before we write the final lines and you close the book, we must give you one more thing that we do that you can implement into your prayer practices. I discovered while sharing on a friend's podcast and during a Wednesday Bible Study Brian and I were asked to lead. The way we pray was new and unheard of for some and garnered quite a bit of response to it.

So, it dawned on me that I must insert it into these pages to be used by ones who are seeking ways to supplement or enrich their prayer lives as well.

It's practical, simple, and meaningful. So, this is what we do, and we hope that it will be a blessing to you as it has been for us. This is our weekly prayer practice. It's a model for us to pray simple, specific, and focused prayers around the things, people and causes that are important to us. So, feel free to use, modify and create your own as is appropriate for you and your family.

> *Sundays-* We pray for each other and our individual selves. Our hearts, health, minds, souls, thoughts, and identities in Christ. We listen for what God is speaking to either of us.
>
> *Mondays-* We pray for our children, our siblings, and our parents. Then, we also pray for our entire family, near and extended.
>
> *Tuesdays-* We pray for our pastors, our church leadership, and the overall church family. We pray for the youth in our lives and for guidance on how to help support, encourage and provoke all to love and good works.
>
> *Wednesdays-* We pray for our secular jobs, our business endeavors, and all our financial resources.

Thursdays- We pray for our city, state, nation and all the nations of this world. We pray for the peace of Jerusalem. In doing so, we include all elected officials, ordinances, policies, and legislation that impact how we work, live and play.

Fridays- We pray for those specific prayers that have been brought to our attention by request or by knowledge of a need.

Saturdays- On the Sabbath, we practice resting and listening only to hear the voice of the Lord. We give concentrated time on this day to actively listen. This is especially helpful in times when there is so much going on.

This is how we do it. I'd just say try it and see if it works for you. You can feel free to send us an email or note and let us know what you think about it or anything else you've read, learned, or thought about this book.

We never know what the world will bring, but what we do know is that we can bring everything to God in prayer.

Knowing Jesus

Okay, so this is not the end just yet. Another very important part of this Christian life is knowing God, accepting Him, and trusting Him with your life. The Bible speaks of there being only one way to the Father and it's through His Son, Jesus Christ. I'd like to introduce Him to you if you will let me. I'm not sure if you got a hold of this book because you're already a believer and part of the family of God (The Body of Christ) or if it was given to you and you're not sure who God really is or maybe you're here and have been wavering a bit, but unsure about a God at all. No matter which group you may fall into, we did not want to close without extending an opportunity for you to make the Lord God, your God.

If there is void that you have been feeling in your heart, only God can fill it for you. It's not about joining our church, but it is about giving your life to the one true God who is the maker of Heaven and Earth. If you want the change in your life that can bring you peace and joy...say this simple prayer:

"Lord Jesus, I ask for your forgiveness of my sins. I believe your son Jesus died and rose again for the cleansing of my sins. I ask that You to come into my heart. I make you my Lord and my Savior today".

If you said that simple prayer, you are now a part of the family of faith. Now, you'll want to get into a Bible based church, join in fellowship and discipleship to know God more personally. Below is the scripture that shares how to accept the gift of salvation God makes available to all of us who will believe. This is the what the Bible says to be saved:

If you declare with your mouth, "Jesus is Lord," and believe in your heart that God raised him from the dead, you will be saved. For it is with your heart that you believe and are justified, and it is with your mouth that you profess your faith and are saved. (Romans 10:9-10 KJV)

The Minister & the Mrs. will be praying for you. We're believing God's very best for you, your spouse, and your family. We'd love to hear from you.

To contact us, write to:
The Minister & The Mrs.
Minister Brian and Michelle Gines
13194 US Highway 301 S
Riverview, FL 33578
Or you can email us at theministerandthemrs@gmail.com.

The Husband's Prayer Requests

Prayer Request	How God Answered	Date

Prayer Request   How God Answered   Date

Prayer Request	How God Answered	Date

The Wife's Prayer Requests

Prayer Request   **How God Answered**   **Date**

Prayer Request	How God Answered	Date

Prayer Request   How God Answered   Date

More from the Author

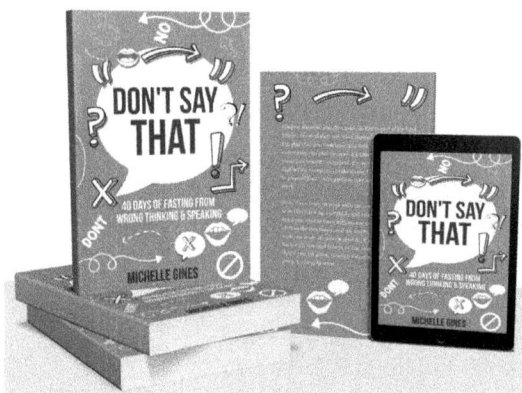

There are no concrete instructions on how to read and relate to this book. Just start reading. You can read one per day, two or three per week or you just might ingest the entire thing in one setting. It doesn't matter. You can read it any way you want to. It's set up as take it one day at a time, just meaning, do your best to fast from these phrases one day at a time.

- Everyday a Phrase or Thought to Fast From with a little biblical wisdom and insight.

- Let's Switch it Up every day I will offer you five ways to think of that phrase differently

– say it differently. It's all about perspective and sometimes we just need to look at it another way. Over time looking at things another way provides an opportunity for an even greater outcome. Every phrase can be removed from your thought life and vocabulary to never be heard from you again. And the great thing about that is you won't miss it at all. I promise you.

• Say it Out Loud. Yes, really, out loud. Why? You need to hear yourself saying something different makes it easier to say it differently if ever you're encountered with that thought. It's good practice.

A good fast from all the junk you might think or say will do the mind and body good! It's time for a fast. Don't Say That will be a game changer – a life changer for you if you'll let it. It won't hurt. And you'll feel better and you'll be glad you did.

979-8-21810-408-5 // $15

Purchase at www.michellegines.online

For Men or Women Struggling with Self-Doubt

Everybody looks at themselves and finds all sorts of reasons not to love what they see, or they wait for someone else to give them permission to love themselves. Like many Christian girls, we listen intently to others' assessment of our lives, situations, and circumstances.

It's time to unlearn everything you have negatively believed about yourself – and retrain your brain to tap into what God says about you and believing that instead!

979-8-47042-179-1 // $15.00

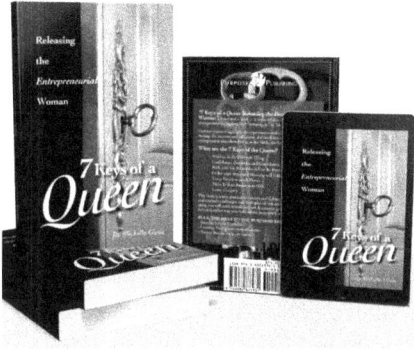

Purchase at www.michellegines.online

Small Business Owner or Want to Be?

"7 Keys of a Queen: Releasing the Entrepreneurial Woman", is not just a book… it is the motivator to every woman entrepreneur struggling with "jumping in" or "sitting on the fence".

This book is practical for any woman that wants to comprehend what entrepreneurship is all about. Everything you will need to make a good decision to get started or move forward; either way you have all the keys you'll need!

PLUS, THE KEYS TO BUSINESS TREASURE CHEST

- Success Secrets Unveiled
- Creating Multiples streams of income
- Tons of Resources to get started.

978-0-98283-793-1 // $15.95

Need Organization for Everything?
Get Spunky, Colorful and Bold

Purchase at www.michellegines.online

The Spunky, Colorful & Bold Collection of Tools to Capture Your Writings for the person who still likes to have a hard copy. Even though the world has gone digital with virtually everything. There are still a few people like us who like good, old fashioned paper & pen.

To that group, The Spunky, Colorful Collection is just for you. This is for the team who likes to coordinate and keep it classy, we've got your pages.

The collection includes 5 Tools for all your habit forming, stress reducing, note capturing stuff with pen ready pages for all of it.

- Dream Journal
- Password Log Book
- Meal Planning Journal
- Notebook
- Self-Care Journal

The simple, easy pages with the vintage matte covers makes the designs functional and fancy.

5 Book Bundle $25 or $6ea